# GENEROUS *Saints*

## Congregations
## Rethinking
## Ethics and Money

## James Hudnut-Beumler

An Alban Institute Publication

Library of Congress Card Number 98-73678

ISBN I-56699-210-9

*For Julia and Adam*

# CONTENTS

Susan Waters is a pastor. She marvels at Eugenia Williams. Eighty-five years old and living mostly on Social Security, Mrs. Williams is nevertheless one of the congregation's five leading givers. Eugenia nurtures relationships, too. She serves as corresponding secretary of the women's association; no sick member fails to receive a card she has picked out. She taught Sunday school 48 Sundays a year for 40 years, missing only the three years she served as a senior volunteer with the Peace Corps in Senegal. Susan wonders if the kind of faith Eugenia Williams demonstrates is a thing of the past. Mrs. Williams is the closest example of a living saint that Susan has ever experienced.

Susan feels that she herself falls far short of Eugenia Williams's kind of sainthood. The money is part of the problem, Susan knows. She and her husband, David, struggle to pay their church pledge. In buying power, their respective salaries as a minister and a high school teacher have declined slightly over the past six years. Meanwhile, the household has gained two children and all the associated expenses. Susan watches other people in the congregation struggle with money, too, but she doesn't know how to talk about the issue. Although some members seem to have all the money they need to take vacations in Europe and Hawaii, one would never know it from their giving to the church.

Susan is a gifted preacher and a conscientious pastor. Under her leadership the church has grown by more than 60 members. Yet the congregation struggles each year to meet its budget. Susan does not understand the choices her members make about using their resources; moreover, she suspects that the members don't understand their own choices either. Last week Susan preached from the Gospel according to John on "abundant life." On her way home she stared out the car

window at falling leaves and wondered, "Do we really know what 'abundant life' is?" What had seemed clear only two hours earlier was now clouded in uncertainty. Stewardship season always brought her doubts to the surface.

\* \* \*

Susan Waters is not an actual person, but I wrote this book for people like her and her congregation. Susan is a composite of many women and men I have met in the past decade who faithfully lead congregations that are experiencing money problems.

I became interested in the topic of generosity in the lives of individual Christians and their congregations by way of three convergent routes. As a program officer at a private foundation, I heard from many leaders—particularly in mainline Protestant denominations—who asserted that American religion was in the midst of an unprecedented financing crisis. As a historian of American religion, I was interested in how things might have changed over the decades. Did people support their churches better in a past era? Did they understand the role of material possessions in their lives better, or at least differently, than we do? Finally, as a Christian who believes that the Gospel reaches to all parts of life, I became convinced that issues involving money are one of the areas where our contemporary congregational life is most troubled.

The more I looked into the so-called financing crisis from these three perspectives, the more I was persuaded that the financial dimension was but a small part of a substantial religious crisis. What to do about material possessions, about money, about work—these are perennial religious issues. How well the people of a particular time meet these issues is a test of their culture and of their faith. In the United States, our understanding of how to live as spiritual beings in a material world has broken down. For example, we volunteer, but we say we do so because it makes us feel good. We tell our children that we donate to charity because it is important to "give something back." We know deep down that wealth will not make us happy; but not knowing how to be happy otherwise, we strive to become rich. Is it any wonder that congregations like Susan Waters's are experiencing multiple crises related to money?

This is a book about money and its place in our lives and in our churches. It is not a book about how to get more money for the work of

the church. I think, however, that better support for the mission of our congregations is one result of becoming clearer in our thinking about money. But I also believe that if we think we can just jump in and talk about stewardship and fund-raising in today's churches, as if all that is needed is to uncover a few new strategies, we are kidding ourselves. The issues surrounding money and Christian discipleship go much deeper.

The time is ripe for congregations to rethink their understandings of how we ought to live faithfully in a material world. The Christian tradition teaches that we are created to be generous in spirit and called to become more holy throughout our lives. The central question of this book therefore involves ethics and money: How shall we live with what we have? Or, as I like to put the same question: How do we live up to our calling to be generous saints?

This book could not have been written without the support and conversation of my colleagues at Columbia Theological Seminary. Jane Harris and Jane Gleim each typed portions of the manuscript and did not hesitate to say which parts were interesting to them. Faculty colleagues Walter Brueggemann, Erskine Clarke, Will Coleman, Charles Cousar, Darrell Guder, Marcia Riggs, Stan Saunders, and George Telford have all been part of substantive conversations with me about the issues engaged in this book. I am lucky to be surrounded by people who trust the Scriptures, have hopes for the church, and know just how much hard work generosity and sainthood are. Above all, I am grateful to my wife, Heidi, for the example of her deep faith and her loving sacrifice to others, not the least to me. I dedicate this book to my children, Julia and Adam, with the hope that they will continue to grow into loving and generous souls, confident in the love of God.

# CHAPTER 1

# *Our Worth Comes from God, Not Money*

The great taboo in contemporary life is money. When we are young, we are told not to discuss it. "Does your mom make a lot of money?" is a much more awkward question during a lull in the Thanksgiving dinner conversation than the innocent query "Where do babies come from?" The taboo continues through adulthood. It is culturally more acceptable to confess to a substance-abuse problem or sexual difficulties than to own up to having overspent one's resources, encountered credit difficulties, or lost employment. The taboo stems from money's central role as an expression and index of worth. Since in a consumer-and-market-oriented society we are what we do, consume, and hoard, we are loath to allow our worth to be compared publicly lest we fail to measure up to others' expectations, much less our own definitions of success.

How much are you worth? How we answer that question says a great deal about what we think of ourselves and about life. In common usage in the American middle class, the question is used to determine an individual's net financial worth. A woman adds up her stocks, bonds, and personal and real property and subtracts debts owed to others—and that is how much she is worth. But suppose we were not so quick to give the conventional answer. To a young child, a mother's or father's net financial worth means not a thing. But the parent's presence at a school performance or at storytime before bed—that's worth something. As most of us look back on the gifts our own parents gave us through relationships, we can see that their value was priceless.

The Christian and Hebrew traditions to which we are heirs have much to say about what we value. People in biblical times demonstrated periodic obsessions with money and material things. When Solomon built his temple, 1 Kings tells us, nearly everything was gold, and everything that was not gold was "costly" stone or wood. The shift is dramatic

from a fairly spiritual valuation of the faith as late as the writing of 2 Samuel to a quantitative valuation of religion. The historian of the Hebrew monarchy knows the price of everything and the value of nothing. Against this background of a loss of values, prophets like Jeremiah and Isaiah and Amos and Hosea emerged to lead the people to a re-appropriation of the values found in the Torah.

Jesus of Nazareth worked within the prophetic tradition. Nearly 1,000 years after Solomon, Jesus addressed followers this way in the Sermon on the Mount: "You cannot serve God and [money]. Therefore I tell you, do not be anxious about your life, what you shall eat or what you shall drink, nor about your body, what you shall put on. Is not life more than food, and body more than clothing?" (Matt. 6:24-25, RSV). He went on to compare the human situation to that of the birds, whom God fed though they neither planted nor harvested, and to the lilies of the field, which were clothed in splendor through no work of their own. Then Jesus asked his hearers, "Are you not of more value than they?" (Matt. 6:26, RSV). The situation Jesus faced was the same as that faced by the Hebrew prophets, the same as the one we face today. Material well-being has become the crushingly dominant value in human life. Not even God stands a chance in the lives of people as long as they prefer the idol of mammon.

Wherever there are taboos, one can be reasonably sure that idols are nearby. The power of the money taboo comes from the fact that we allow so few countervailing forces to influence our lives. When people have but one central operative value, they guard it carefully and surround it with mystery and taboo, lest that one value be taken away.

## Putting Money in Its Place

This chapter is about putting money in its rightful place. Many figures in Christian history have sought to do away with material concerns, arguing that they have no place in the life of the godly. I think that this quixotic impulse does more harm than good, for we are material beings as well as spiritual selves. Denying one's materiality is like pretending that one does not have a body. Stop eating and drinking, and soon one falls victim to the very reality one sought to deny. In the same discourse we considered a moment ago, Jesus recognized this fact when he countered the questions "What shall we eat?" and "What shall we wear?" with the assurance that "your heavenly Father knows that you need them

all" (Matt. 6:31-32, RSV). So being faithful to God as one's ultimate value means reducing the importance of money and other forms of material wealth in our lives. It also means increasing the importance of values like generosity, compassion, and love that come from placing our ultimate reliance on God alone.

When money ceases to be an idol, the taboo that forbids talking about money begins to erode. Why? Because the power of an idol lies in its ability to hurt us if we displease it. Yet even when dethroned, money is worth talking about. Saying that we are of infinite worth in God's eyes, while true, does not actually help much with cold, hard reality. Similarly, counsels to perfection encourage people to give up, since they will never attain the mountaintop of expected behavior. One way to think about money is as an outward sign of an inward state. How we make our money and what we will (and will not) spend it on make a witness to others about who we are. Our spending choices also stand as a witness to ourselves, since the tendency toward self-deception is a key dimension of the human condition. Examining our own spending helps us to begin breaking through this self-deception about our values.

If faithful obedience and love of God are our ultimate value, we need to start talking about how other things in our lives relate to that value. Indeed, in the case of money, it becomes crucial to talk about it in the light of our ultimate commitments. If we do not talk about money and its place in our lives, we might easily make only a verbal commitment to following in the way of God, while behaviorally leaving money in its privileged and protected space. Either we allow our discipleship to Jesus Christ to affect our relation to money or money will affect our relationship to Christ.

## Getting Over the Insecurities

Christian congregations have an important role to play in helping us get over the destructive power of money so that we can put it in its proper place and live the more abundant lives God intended for us. What is a congregation when it comes to finances but a collection of people who behave in fairly insecure ways around issues of money? Until we discipline our use of things to accord consistently with our spiritual understanding of ourselves, we are congregations of individuals whose money

practices will keep us "acting out" toward one another out of our insecurities—by which I don't mean just psychological maladaptations. Rather I mean our natural responses to the existential realities we find unsettling and hard to accept. We can never have enough money, love, or health. Death is a certainty. These facts of life make us insecure. But whether we can master our insecurities sufficiently to have an abundant life is the test of our character as individuals and as congregations.

Think about a congregation in the way one might think about a kindergarten. Every kindergartener starts the year as a bundle of insecurities. Every child needs to know, *really know*, that he or she is accepted. Acceptance of oneself, one's peers, and the things one can't change is the work of the kindergarten. We like to think that these insecurities go away, but they merely transmute themselves, and we become better at masking them. My basic point is this: congregations also have the task of helping members master their insecurities and find acceptance and in turn provide it to others.

The way money is linked directly and indirectly to powerful insecurities was brought home to me when my daughter, Julia, was four years old and in a prekindergarten program at Emory University's on-campus church. I was preparing dinner when Julia walked across the kitchen floor in a hurry and dropped a plastic sandwich bag full of pennies and silver coins. "What's going on?" I asked, figuring it was part of a game. Julia broke down in tears: "Michael and Eric told me that they were going to kill me if I didn't bring them money tomorrow. Eric's father has a gun, and they said they'd bring it to school and use it on me unless I brought them money every day." From an early age, then, we learn that money is linked to power, and that power is linked to violence or the threat of violence.

As children we learn also that money is a source of things that make us happy. For my part, I still remember my brother John going to the dime store with me and our middle brother, Steve, when he was three or four years old and allowed to pay for his own candy choice for the first time. "John, show the woman your candy," Steve said. "Now hand her the money, and she will give you change." John paid with a five-dollar bill for perhaps 20 cents' worth of candy. Not having learned the differences in the denominations of bills and coins, he was delighted to receive four bills and an assortment of coins in change from the clerk. When we went to the dime store a week later, John had both a dime

(enough to pay for his candy) and a dollar bill. He insisted on paying with the dollar bill. We asked him why. "Because," he said, "that way I get more money back and I can buy more candy." My brother thought he had discovered the financial fountain of youth. Not only could he acquire candy, but in doing so he could also increase the stock of funds with which to buy more candy. Being older brothers, we quickly and ruthlessly disabused John of his fantastic discovery. We fixed upon that preschooler our six- and eight-year-old (and nearly adult) insecurities about money, that scarce resource linked to happiness.

Looking back, I am amazed at how these sentimental lessons about money, instilled early, stay with us over the years. As in most other areas of faith and life in which we are particularly troubled, we are collectively the victims of basic insecurities brought forward unchecked. Still, I think we can learn something from how other insecurities, dealt with earlier, apply to healing our insecurities about money. A good kindergarten doesn't just manage insecurities. Rather it leads its members into new appreciation of one another. Such statements as "Jordan can paint a beautiful daisy" and "Sarah is a good friend to Jamie when she is sad" are the building blocks of self-esteem and mutual understanding. Jordan and Sarah feel good about themselves, and others in the class are led to see something new and noble in Jordan and Sarah.

Churches can do that too. Indeed, being the body of Christ means that we are supposed to do that for one another—and applaud one another not only to build self-esteem but also to help us get past the big adult blocks of money, mortality, morality, and vocation. In Paul's metaphor of the body, we are called to see assets in one another's diversity. All too often, we see ourselves as the sum of our individual insecurities and disabilities. Insecurities about money can undo us, but they don't have to. Yet how can congregations help with these insecurities when they won't even discuss the issue?

One basic issue about congregational life boils down to this: Is the church to be a bartender or a therapist to its members? A bartender may adopt the posture of a confessor, but he can offer only drinks and a ready ear. The therapist, on the other hand, is oriented not only toward listening to foibles and insecurities but also toward helping the client do something about them. Too often contemporary churchgoers don't want to be healed, just heard. Or perhaps, more accurately, we wish to be healed and forgiven without being challenged, changed, or asked to repent.

## To Know and Be Known

The healthy congregation is one in which members know enough about one another to truly help shoulder burdens in adversity and celebrate joys in times of blessing. Given the way money intersects with our identities, relationships, and struggles, congregations must become places where it is safe for us to be known (even as regards our money) if they are to help us live into an acceptance of God's grace.

Still, there are within the church apologists for keeping the money taboo in place. These people argue that not even the pastor should know how much money people make or give to the church; otherwise he or she will be tempted to court the rich members or allow levels of giving to determine the quality of pastoral service that individuals receive. The argument is intelligible at some level. Ministers are sinful too. And it follows that they may pay more attention to those who have been generous to the church and, by extension, to the church's minister. But the argument seems to suggest that money is the only area where in-depth knowledge might distort the pastor-parishioner relationship. It may be that knowing someone is not generous could provide pastoral insight into an aspect of weak discipleship in the parishioner's life.

To see how flawed the arguments are for maintaining the taboo, one has only to substitute other conditions into the argument. Read the following statements aloud and ask whether they make moral sense:

> *A minister should not know if a man is abusing his wife, because it will undermine the pastor's ability to serve the husband pastorally.*

> *Ministers should not know about a pattern of alcohol or drug abuse in a member's life because knowing that will diminish the person in the eyes of the pastor.*

The fact that so many, including ministers, believe that deep insight into people's lives should stop at the threshold of money and finances suggests that we are in fact giving money too large a place in life. Indeed, I would argue that ministers are only the first people who should know about the material condition of the church's individual members. The real source of the taboo about money is the desire to withhold something

about ourselves from our brothers and sisters. The money taboo has roots both in contemporary culture and in deep religious, but non-Christian, understandings of the relation of money to human worth.

Does it not seem odd that a finance officer at a car dealership can acquire within 15 minutes information about our finances, wealth, reliability, and foibles that our pastors will never know in a lifetime of relationship? Perhaps it is because we feel dehumanized by the functional relationship with a car dealer and prefer to keep one place in our lives—our congregations—where we are not judged by how much wealth we have or how quickly we pay our bills. More likely, we want desperately to be forgiven without having to confess who we really are and what we have done and failed to do. We would thereby convert our churches and their pastors into instruments of what German theologian Dietrich Bonhoeffer called "cheap grace." The most distressing dimension of being known for who we are is not that we don't want to come clean (though that is bad enough) but rather that we don't really believe we would be forgiven and accepted if our inward selves were exposed.

An insurance agent named Steve became a candidate for the ministry. Steve told his story this way: "I knew as an insurance agent that half the people I met would sit across the desk from me and lie. I learned that I needed to be in a place where people could and would tell the truth and be accepted for who they are." I hope that Steve's experience as a minister is better than his life as an insurance agent. I suspect it will be, for our churches are places that are better than most for allowing us to be known so that we might be transformed. Still, certain factors suggest that Steve will encounter barriers to full disclosure with his church members. The typical bourgeois American church projects a veneer of "niceness." The people in the pew next to us appear never to have money troubles, self-doubt, vocational uncertainty, or purpose-of-life problems.

There are two exceptions—personal health and the health of loved ones. The only time the veneer of niceness comes down is when it is inescapable because we have cancer or our child is ill or a parent has died. By contrast, it is possible to go for months in a typical church without knowing about a divorce. Is this because our churches are judgmental? Yes, but it is also due to the absence of moral blame attached (in most cases) to illness. And that brings us to the religious-cultural factors that lead to our twisted understandings, beliefs, and practices surrounding

money. The Scriptures remind us that God's rain falls on the just and
unjust alike, but the tendency is real for popular and preached religion
to assign moral superiority to those who prosper. "As a man thinketh, so
shall he prosper" is an important and dangerous text in this war of religious outlooks between those who believe that riches follow righteousness and those who do not. (It also turns out to be dangerous in the sense
that it sounds so much like the Bible that people just assume that's where
it comes from.)

Once we start down the road of understanding economic success as
the reward for hard work and virtue, we are well on the way to understanding wealth and income as signs of God's favor. What person, given
this understanding of God's favor "index," would like to stand up in
church and publicly proclaim, "I'm an $18,000-a-year stock clerk at the
hardware store"? We might talk about the functions of our jobs, but we
are not going to disclose the salary for that work (even though most
people could venture a realistic guess). The proud secretly congratulate
themselves for doing well by the world's standards. The timid and shy
are grateful that no one knows how little they make and that they are not
judged. Both groups commit the sin of seeing themselves as the world
sees them and valuing themselves according to the amount of money
they earn and the assets they amass.


## Becoming Generous

But there's another reason for our desire to keep our financial affairs
quiet. We would like to think that the money we have belongs to us, and
to us alone. We fear that letting our brothers and sisters know what we
have opens the way for us to be compelled to share it with others. We
say about our giving to the church, for example, "That decision is between God and me." What we mean is "It's my money, and I'll decide
what to do with it without your help, thank you." We fear that like the
government and its despised Internal Revenue Service, the church,
knowing that our income is $50,000, will levy a 10 percent tax on the
funds.

I favor sharing information about individual resources not so that
the churches can coerce their tithe more easily. Rather it is my goal to
enable Christians to be more generous people. Generosity is a spiritual

disposition, not a quantifiable percentage of income. Three hundred
years before Jesus lived, the Greek philosopher Aristotle laid out the
classical understanding of generosity as an absolute matter. Only the
wealthy could be generous, because only the wealthy were in a position
to provide a large gift to the public. Jesus turned that classical reasoning
about generosity on its head by calling attention to the widow's mite:
"Truly I tell you, this poor widow has put in more than all of them; for
all of them have contributed out of their abundance, but she out of her
poverty has put in all she had to live on" (Luke 21:3-4, RSV). Ever since,
the Western tradition has made room for the idea that there is something
about the disposition of the giver that accounts for the quality of the gift.
Generosity is the virtue that emerges as the antidote for money's destructive grip on our lives and spirits. Generosity emerges from gratitude.
Open-hearted gratitude is what motivated the widow, while those who
"gave from their abundance" were still holding something back.

Our most beloved stories in the West tend to involve the virtues of
generosity and selflessness and their opposite vices of greed and selfish-
ness. Think back over the Bible stories you learned as a child. The conflict between Cain and Abel involves jealousy over God's favor toward
each brother's line of work. Lot and Abraham split over property and
labor disputes. It is Abraham who, by looking at God's larger picture,
finally prospers. It is the gift of paternal favor in the form of a coat of
many colors that leads Joseph's brothers to sell him into slavery, and it
is their lack of material subsistence that brings them back to him.

The stories told by Jesus are frequently about money and its many
substitutes. A man builds bigger barns to increase his prosperity, only to
discover that he is to die that very night. A Samaritan proves himself to
be a true neighbor by sharing his resources to care for another.

Perhaps the most striking of Jesus' stories is that of the rich man
and Lazarus (Luke 16:19-30). "There was a rich man who was dressed
in purple and fine linen and who feasted sumptuously every day," said
Jesus. "And at his gate lay a poor man named Lazarus, covered with
sores, who longed to satisfy his hunger with what fell from the rich man's
table; even the dogs would come and lick his sores." Both men died.
Lazarus was carried by angels to be with Abraham. The rich man went
to Hades, where he burned in agony. Noting the reversal of fortunes, he
called out to father Abraham to send Lazarus with water. "No," Abraham
replied, "there is an unbridgeable chasm between you and Lazarus."

"Then," the rich man begged, "send him to my father's house—for I have five brothers—that he may warn them, so that they will not also come into this place of torment." Abraham replied, "They have Moses and the prophets; they should listen to them." The rich man said, "No, father Abraham; but if someone goes to them from the dead, they will repent." Abraham shut him up, saying, "If they do not listen to Moses and the prophets, neither will they be convinced even if someone rises from the dead." Clearly, some people will never get it.

Not only in the Bible do we find these stories. Indeed, where would Shakespeare be without tales of the generous and miserly? Traditional folklore also provides commentary on human generosity and its absence. In one of the most famous of the Eastern European Baba Yaga stories, an old women is asked by a starving soldier passing by to make him some bread. She agrees, but each time her bread turns out bigger and better than any loaf she has baked previously, she selfishly insists on baking yet another (and presumably inferior) loaf. The final result is that she smothers herself with the ultimate loaf, all for fear of giving away a good loaf to a beggar.

O. Henry's famous short story "The Gift of the Magi" brings the generosity-tale genre into our century as Della sells her beautiful knee-length hair to buy a platinum fob chain for her husband Jim's watch, while he sells his watch to purchase the pure tortoise-shell combs with jeweled rims Della had admired in a Broadway jeweler's window. Rather than finding such an exchange pointless, the couple and the readers see in the gifts the model of selfless romantic love. Della and Jim don't end up with useless gifts; they realize the greater gift of love.

We hear in these stories recurring moral themes: It is better to be a good poor person than to court riches and worldly favor. Acts of real kindness are valuable no matter how small (or, as we like to say, "It's the thought that counts"). The rich and powerful are corrupted by their largesse. Money cannot buy happiness. Turning your back on your family or other people will catch up with you. Sacrifice for others is rewarded either in this world or in the eyes of God. These are the messages we preserve in our faith and our literary traditions. We tell and retell these stories to ennoble ourselves and our children. We tell these tales to preserve a vision of the good life.

Generosity begins with connecting what we see as noble in others to our own lives. Just as the rich man had Moses and the prophets, we too

are surrounded by the cultural materials from which to craft lives of generosity. Yet instead of making a connection between the stories we embrace and our lives, which are dominated by money, we allow a disconnect to occur. It is as though we think accounts of lives well lived are charming but impractical, as though we believe money is finally the rule by which we must live. When we don't share our personal money stories with our pastors and trusted others, we withhold a part of ourselves with which others could help us. Then again, we don't even realize that we need help. God knows we all need clothing, yet shopping as a form of self-expression is an addiction for many in our churches. Vacationing, eating out, and enjoying gourmet foods are all part of living "the good life" in our time, but all too often they become our version of obsessing over "What shall I eat?" when more delight- and grace-filled forms of living with God and neighbor are possible.

## Where to Begin

That we don't talk about money doesn't mean that we don't worry about it. In fact, most Americans worry about it constantly. Are we saving enough? Will Social Security be there for us when we are old? Will our aging parents in nursing homes clean us out just in time to prevent us from sending our children to college? Will our children take care of us? Can we afford a new car? Can we afford repairs on the old car? Where will next month's mortgage payment come from? Read over the list. Most people keep such worries to themselves, or share them only with marital partners. Sometimes, when the partners disagree, we turn to a coworker for understanding, but rarely to a pastor or to the church and its members.

I think that one of the best ways people can be the church together in a money-dominated age is to break the taboo against discussing money and money worries. If we are concerned with having enough money to care for others or ourselves, or with meeting payments, let us confess those concerns to our brothers and sisters in a supportive setting. A burden confessed is a burden shared.

If we are going to talk about money in the context of our congregations, we owe something to each other—the discipline of going to the next level in listening. One is tempted, when someone relates a financial

problem, or a family problem with a financial dimension, or a job-related problem, to try to help that person find a quick fix. What most of us need is not a quick fix or even a good coping strategy. For most of us, a money-related problem is the tip of the iceberg. Underneath the worry about Social Security is worry about growing old. Will I keep my independence, my friends, my mental capacities? Will I be able to buy the help, if I need it, of people I can trust? Below the issue of how to pay for college is concern for the welfare of one's children. Will they be happy? Will they choose important and satisfying work? Will they be able to get by without parental protection? What Christians need to do for each other is to engage their brothers and sisters at below-the-surface levels.

The place to begin is with leading people to say what's in their hearts and then following up the Social Security comment (to cite but one example) with a question related to hopes and fears about aging. The prime American value of autonomy will make us want to deflect such questions. "No," we will want to say, "I know exactly what to do as long as I've got enough money." The tragedy of this presumption of autonomy is that we cut ourselves off from the very conversations about our hopes and fears and insecurities in the world and before God with which our faith communities are in a position to help us.

Congregations of Christians can do other things to counter the power of money in our lives. The church's ministry to its members is not merely problem-centered. We also can tell the stories of our lives in less materialistic ways. If we truly believe that life is more than bread and water (and clothing, houses, and cars), then the church must be the institution that validates our nonmaterial values. How? By telling the stories of the generous saints in our midst.

An example: A man's child is dying of cancer. He takes family leave without pay to tend to the child. The cancer abates for a while, but returns. The man's employer replaces him at the end of the statutory leave period. The child dies at home one evening. Now, what does the congregation say in public? What do members say in private to the man who lost a job for the child he loved? Too often we just say, "Sorry for your loss." Privately, we may even say to each other, "It's too bad that cost him his job."

These weak responses are not adequate to the followers of Jesus Christ. Someone needs to stand up and say in the presence of the congregation: "Henry, we grieve with you, but we are also proud of you, for

you gave of yourself to your daughter in her time of greatest need without reserve. You are a witness to us all that people come first. We say that nothing can separate us from the love of God; you showed us all the love of God made real through your steadfast commitment to Sarah. Now, Henry, in the name of Jesus Christ, we promise to stand by you in love as you grieve and as you begin to put your life back together. We'll help you find a job, and for my part, I'm going to pay your electric bill until you're back on your feet."

If this fictional speech seems too personal for your church, it suggests how far we have to go in most congregations to reconcile ourselves to Gospel values. The way to encourage generosity is to recognize it publicly and to support those who display its virtues.

The people of God know something that others don't. They know that their worth comes from God and not from money—not from money earned, hoarded, spent to purchase things, or used to exercise power. Once people see this truth, they can see that they have things going for them, for they are gifted with an abundance of skills and stories, with opportunities for love and service, and with one another. The people of God know that they have things money cannot buy; they know they are rich in things of the soul. The job of the contemporary congregation is, as always, to increase love and understanding of God and love toward the neighbor. Lest money stand in the way of love, congregations must become places where the abundant gifts of God to the people of God become known and celebrated.

## Exercises

In the two exercises that follow, Christians are encouraged to uncover the hidden sources of meaning and value that inform their lives.

### Constructing Our Worth

This exercise challenges you to construct a statement of your worth. Financial planners tell us to add up our financial assets and liabilities to construct a statement of net worth. By contrast, this exercise asks you to state who you are apart from the things you possess. On one side of a

divided sheet of paper list the things that you have and value. Pay special attention to relationships, skills, knowledge, habits, and practices that help define who you are and what you do, like, and have to offer others.

On the other side of the sheet, list what debts you owe others, including God. Give attention to how you acquired the relationships, skills, knowledge, habits, and practices you listed as assets. Are there any residuals—that is, items of value that you acquired without incurring a debt in some way to someone else? Discuss your statement of worth with another individual who has also completed the exercise. What do you hear in your partner's self-description? What does your partner hear in yours?

### What Are Our Assets?

This second exercise is an extension of the first, but for a community of believers. It consists of answering the question, "What human resources would we have if we had no money?" The most helpful way to approach this exercise of identifying community assets is to encourage individuals to speak not for themselves but for others. That is, instead of John's identifying what he brings to the group, members of the group affirm what they see as John's actual and potential contributions. Then John reflects on what others have said about him. Someone from the group should record the highlights of the member's nonfinancial assets. Finally, once the group's assets have been identified, group members should discuss what they learned in the exercise.

In some ways, the second exercise is like a group-survival task. Answering the question "Can we get out of the woods?" is one way of discovering just how adequate our resources are. If we are confident that we will have what we need under life-threatening circumstances, we are more apt to let go of irrational fears. Outward Bound and other outdoor-survival programs know this fact about human beings and structure their learning experiences around allowing groups to come to terms with the apparent absence of customary tools for problem-solving. For a church group, particularly a church group that has been stressed out over budget matters, it is helpful to identify the community's resources apart, for the time being, from its financial resources. Money is, of course, important to a congregation's functioning, but people are often surprised to see how much they have going for themselves apart from their money.

CHAPTER 2

# *God's Big Economy (and Our Small Ones)*

The greatest block to generosity is insecurity. It is hard to be a giving person when you think that there may not be enough for you. Insecurity is driven in turn by uncertainty and scarcity. It is the unexamined assumptions in life that most often prove to be our undoing. Everyone has a stake in the economy, but few seek to understand it. One of the fundamental barriers to becoming generous and saintly in our material and spiritual lives is our failure to come to terms with the large-scale reality of the economy in ways that square with our calling to be God's people. As long as we allow the engine that produces the means to live to remain shrouded in mystery, we are slaves to uncertainty and insecurity. Our goal in this chapter, therefore, is to lay bare one of the most basic questions about collective human interaction: What is an economy for, anyway? Once that question is posed, we can reframe it with God in mind: If this is God's world, then what is the purpose of an economy and what does that tell us about the way we ought to order our lives?

We only have to tune in to the media to see how the question of purpose gets lost in the shuffle of economic news. The question posed by *Time, Newsweek,* CNN, and our daily newspapers, perhaps most of all by *USA Today,* is "How is the economy doing?" (by which of course most media really mean the U.S. economy in isolation from the rest of the world). The question is posed as though there are but two answers. Either the economy is doing well or it is doing poorly. (Perhaps here would be a good place to insert a *USA Today* graphic with sunny faces for a growing economy and frowning umbrellas for one in decline.) It is possible, however, that from my perspective as a stockholder, the economy is doing exceedingly well *and* that from my perspective as a wage earner, the economy leaves much to be desired. In fact, this is the situation in which many members of our churches find themselves today.

It is a sad commonplace of contemporary middle-class life that the same interoffice mail that brings a quarterly statement from the employer's 401(k) plan with a 12 percent gain in our account balance may also bring a notice that we have been downsized out of a job. The simple class divisions of people into the categories of workers and owners no longer adequately describe the participants in the contemporary economy. It is possible to be both a winner and a loser in today's economy.

## Contemporary Market Ideology

There is perhaps no system of thought at work in the world today more powerful than market capitalism. Market mechanisms for buying and selling goods and services go back in human history at least as far as the bazaar in the ancient Near East. Capitalism, as a highly efficient mode of production linked to wealth formation, is a more recent phenomenon. Working together, relatively free of governmental encumbrances, capitalism and market mechanisms have remade the face of the globe. Market capitalism is the true winner in the fight against communism in Eastern Europe and the Soviet Union. It has created substantial new wealth in the "little dragons" of East Asia and Korea, which less than half a century ago suffered grinding poverty, feudalism, and an extractive economy controlled by European and American imperialists. Everywhere it goes, market capitalism brings consumer goods, but also a measure of economic freedom that carries a corollary human freedom to express one's individuality and to profit from one's activity.

The market economy is the engine of contemporary global change—a powerful force for expression, innovation, and alas, for domination. Something powerful always creates the potential for idolatry, and market capitalism is often idolized in the contemporary world. After all, the market cannot give us some of the goods we need in life. The efficient production and sale of material things (goods in one sense) will not give us family, happiness, friendship, self-expression, and spiritual nourishment (goods in another, more important sense). It is said, "You can never get enough of a substitute." Why? Because a substitute always leaves you hungry for the real thing. The soft drink Coca-Cola was wisely positioned in advertisements as "The Real Thing" and later as an eternal verity, "Always Coca-Cola," for its image-makers and marketers under-

stood that all human thirst exceeds a simple desire for flavored sugar-water. The nature of human beings is to look for meaning and happiness wherever we may find them. But it is also the human plight to be, as the country-western song affirms, "looking for love in all the wrong places."

This human propensity to seek our meaning in commerce is an old story. Consider the people the prophet Amos met in his marketplace. Amos 8 contains these words:

> Hear this, you that trample on the needy,
> and bring to ruin the poor of the land,
> saying, "When will the new moon be over
> so that we may sell grain;
> and the sabbath,
> so that we may offer wheat for sale?
> We will make the ephah small and the shekel great,
> and practice deceit with false balances,
> buying the poor for silver
> and the needy for a pair of sandals,
> and selling the sweepings of the wheat" (Amos 8:4-6).

Look over those words again. They are actually only Amos's windup, his description of the people to whom the words of God will be addressed.

Are we terribly different from those eighth-century B.C.E. Jews? Amos addressed a group of people who were obsessed by business. All other values, and particularly compassion for the poor, were swept aside for the sake of the trade, the sale, the deal. The eighth-century traders could "make a market" in anything. The poor? How about one pair of new sandals for one old widow? They did not know where to stop. They even gathered up the sweepings of the wheat for sale. The offense here was that the "sweepings" were leftover grain that was by law and custom to be left behind and kept out of the market so that gleaners, those without normal market access, could forage for food to sustain life. In short, Amos decried a practice not unlike that of criminalizing a homeless person's searching for food in restaurant dumpsters. The law does not preserve the health of the homeless or even the community so much as it preserves the convenience and exclusive food franchise of restaurants and grocers.

Are we so terribly different from Amos's business-obsessed people?

I don't think so. More than a half-century ago, President Calvin Coolidge put it memorably: "The business of America is business." And most of the time, working Americans, and particularly middle-class Americans, act as if Coolidge were 100 percent correct. The true "business" of America, like that of any other land, is more than doing business in the strict commercial sense of the word. Oh, to be sure, we need commercial activity; we need to exchange goods and services. But life is about more than making, fixing, buying, and selling. The business (in the sense of what we are to do—our busyness) of America is also about having babies, playing music, worshiping, serving others, tending our homes, and laughing with friends, among a myriad of things. The true business of America is living, and living together. In Amos's time and in our own, human priorities tend to become confused. Why do we let commerce crowd out our other values and life pursuits? The answer in a word is "scarcity."

Anyone who remembers anything from a college economics class probably remembers two things—the law of supply and demand and the classic definition of economics as the science of the distribution of scarce resources. Scarcity. The natural human response to the world is to believe that there is not enough to go around and to act according to that belief. We are scarcity people. The Genesis creation account of 1:1-2:3 was produced for just such a people. They had been living with hunter-gatherer scarcity and now were having great trouble adapting to the condition of agrarian/urban abundance. They lived in the time of the kings, between the rise of the Davidic monarchy and its collapse with the exile to Babylon. To them the priestly writers (writer-editors working approximately 750 years B.C.E.) needed to say that God made everything and it was abundant, good, and enough. In contrast to the older tradition of Genesis 2:4-25, in the priestly account human beings are late to the creation party. Everything is good and ready before God introduces humankind made in God's image. And so it is that on the sixth day God blesses the human creatures, male and female, and says to them:

> See, I have given you every plant yielding seed that is upon the face of all the earth, and every tree with seed in its fruit; you shall have them for food. And to every beast of the earth, and to every bird of the air, and to everything that creeps on the earth, everything that

has the breath of life, I have given every green plant for food (Gen. 1:29-30).

What follows the sixth day in this account of the creation is important. For human beings and God, the seventh day is for rest. Like the sweepings left behind for the poor, time is to be left unprogrammed by Jews that they may recognize that six days are enough for work and that all they have is ultimately a gift from God. The seven-day-a-week economy is an offense to the Creator, for it never stops to recognize that the human creature is neither the source nor the sole end of the created order.

God's sovereignty over creation permeates the Hebrew Scriptures. Whether one turns to the Law, the prophets, or the wisdom literature, God is in control and sanctioning human activity. The Psalms put it this way: "The earth is the Lord's and the fulness thereof" (Ps. 24:1, RSV). That phrase, "fulness thereof," sounds to us like an Elizabethan throwaway line, an empty heaping of words. In fact, the old language preserves the Hebraic sense quite nicely to emphasize Yahweh's total ownership. The world is God's, says the psalmist, who, anticipating the objection, "Yeah, but what about my stuff?" shoots back with words that leave no room for doubt. There is no "my stuff." Everything is in God's domain. This insight is the beginning of the insight that God's economy is larger than all other contenders for the title "the economy."

We have trouble accepting the news that everything is in God's domain. We have even more trouble with the idea of Sabbath rest. The average American worker works eight hours a week more than did his or her counterpart two decades ago. We love to tell each other how hard we work. Many of the new technologies actually function not to free us from drudgery but to allow us to work in more places and at more times. Automatic washing machines freed our mothers from hours of menial work each week. Now we do the laundry while we are doing other tasks. Pagers, laptop computers, and cell phones tether us to work so that work can find us when we are with our friends and loved ones. The much-heralded changes in worker productivity have come largely at the cost of a loss in personal time. Yet even when we give ourselves over to work, there are no guarantees that our work will make us secure, let alone love us back.

## The Story of Gordon and Anne

Gordon and Anne Moore considered themselves lucky. They had met
soon after each graduated from college, when both were working on
Wall Street. Anne worked her way up from broker's assistant to broker.
Gordon managed to move up even further and found himself overseeing
a staff of 20 bond salesmen. The financial rewards were not as high as
those of a successful bond salesman, but the money was steady and quite
good. Moreover, the risks of a bad year were low. Besides, both Gordon
and Anne were more service- than aggressively sales-oriented people.

After their first child was born, Anne decided to stay home, and
they moved to a community in New Jersey that reminded both of them
of the Midwestern suburbs in which they had grown up. The American
dream had been good to Gordon and Anne. Through a couple of market
corrections, Gordon still received bonuses and promotions. Two more
children came along, together with vacations, braces, and a $100,000
kitchen/family room addition, which brought their house up to neighborhood standards. Then Gordon's luck at work changed. His firm merged
with another. His boss made out very well because of an equity stake in
the firm worth enough to convert into early retirement at age 46. Gordon
had only two years of unexercised stock options to his credit. Worse yet,
as the boss explained to him, Gordon wouldn't have a job after the sales
operations consolidated.

"What did I do wrong?" he asked.

"Nothing," his boss replied. "But let's face facts, Gordon. Management has decided to keep the younger supervisors. They're hungry,
they're cheaper, and they've still got something to prove. Look, Gordon,
it's not that you did anything wrong. It's just that if they want growth,
they've got to have a world-beater."

Five thousand dollars a month after taxes. That's what Gordon and
Anne had to bring in to keep the house with its two mortgages, taxes,
and the usual expenses. There weren't a lot of $100,000-a-year jobs for
middle managers in the financial industry after October 1987. Gordon
and Anne's carefully assembled life in the suburbs was falling apart
around them.

From the moment she stopped working full time and delivered her
child, Anne's life had revolved around the church. A mothers-in-transition
group helped her make the adjustment to stay-at-home mother. The

church's preschool was her children's first experience of friends and formal education. She served as a deacon and later as an elder. She brought her energies to restructuring the church's Christian education effort, and even pinch-hit when the church was between ministers of education. Acknowledged workers, even leaders in the church, Gordon and Anne found their association with this fellowship threatened by the fact that when their savings ran out they would have to move to an apartment more than ten miles away.

More painful still was the feeling that people were talking behind their backs. They felt that people regarded them as losers in a community of the successful. Indeed, church members, partly to reassure themselves that the Moores' fate could not befall them, would whisper among themselves. "Poor Anne," they said. "She's so wonderful. To think that they may lose all they've got. Gordon's a nice man, but it's a hard business unless you're ambitious and willing to make a lot of family sacrifices to stay on top."

I have observed this dynamic in a variety of communities. I consider it a tragic misfortune that I've seen enacted so often since 1980— the phenomenon of families forced from their homes and even, by extension, their churches by the loss of the primary wage earner's job. It is tragic that the fellowship of the body of Christ is premised, in some congregations, upon the ability to maintain a certain lifestyle.

The Christian church in the United States is predicated to a remarkable degree on a congregation's ability to pay for its ministry. Roman Catholics, who thought they were different, that their parishes were territorial and ubiquitous, first learned in Detroit in the early 1980s (and later in other dioceses) that even Catholics danced to the money piper's tune as Archbishop Edmund Szoka marked particular parish churches for closure. Protestant churches in this city and others had been closing for years, all because congregations lacked the resources to sustain their ministries.

Our churches can do little to change economic reality on the macro level. Plant closings, unchecked suburban growth, and population booms and busts are not trends that the church in its ordinary operations can affect. Yet at the micro level, at the level of the congregation, we can do much to live in the broader economy constituted by God and not only in the economy as narrowly construed by those who measure employment, prices, and interest rates.

Congregations can be substitutes for the country club, or they can serve as a witness to God's alternative economy. That is, they can accept and affirm the status quo, or they can place what seem to be given realities in a larger moral framework that calls into question the debilitating assumptions of the status quo. The church's message to the world is that there is much more to life than meets the eye. God's alternative economy is, if we will let it be, more real than the closed-universe economy in which we constantly feel ourselves to be trapped. Living in the alternative economy begins with recognizing that human worth is only partly engaged by the narrower version of the economy as workplace and marketplace.

When Gordon and Anne lost their accustomed place in the economy, the burden fell upon their congregation to demonstrate that it stood with them in solidarity. Perhaps this demonstration takes as radical a form as helping them with money to maintain their housing for a time, or taking the family into another church member's home. At the least it means an affirmation of all that this family means to the congregation beyond Gordon's job and their financial contribution. This affirmation may take several forms. One might be to establish child-care networking with other families so that both adults can work for pay. Another might be to recognize publicly the work Anne has done in caring for children —her own and those of the congregation. Still another might be to give Gordon and other displaced workers opportunities to demonstrate their worth in mission-related service sponsored by the church and directed to brothers and sisters even less fortunate than Gordon and Anne.

These suggestions may sound like sending people who have no income to work without pay. But consider the usual alternative whereby we say, in effect, "Go and get a real job, and then come back and volunteer some time. We don't need to see you around here until you're back on your feet, for now you have nothing of worth to contribute." It may mean that when Gordon and Anne need to move to an apartment, a large number of congregation members will move them for free. Again the liberating insight is this: not every good thing costs money.

All of these hypothetical demonstrations of Christian solidarity in times of economic distress will make middle-class Americans feel somewhat squeamish. We are used to keeping economic matters to ourselves and solving them at the level of the family or the individual. One thing is clear about the coming years in the globalized American economy,

however, and that is that more and more people will find themselves undervalued and displaced by the marketplace. American congregations will need to learn better to meet the needs of their people in these situations. Congregations have untapped gifts for living in the greater reality of God's economy when the ostensible economy is harming their members. Individuals are weak, but congregations are rarely so. Just as with creation, so it is with congregations: there is enough to go around. And the first step toward meeting personal insecurity with congregational strength may be to bring the whole mess before God.

Suppose that rather than allowing our out-of-work or struggling members to suffer in silent humiliation, we prayed to God on their behalf as if we meant it, as if the suffering of one of us truly diminished all of us. If our congregations were willing to own our troubles before God in prayer, would it be long before we shared those troubles as the undone work of the congregational community? Where there is no confession, there is no awareness that can lead to transformation and healing. But when a group of believing people place a sincere concern before God, it usually follows that they will try to address that concern as best they can. If we pray for ten members who need work, will we stop with prayer alone? Yet even here, there is opportunity for growth if we learn that work is more than jobs alone. Just as with our view of economy, our theological conception of work needs to be enlarged and enriched.

## Why Do We Work?

Western anthropologists in the early part of the 20th century visited traditional societies all over the world. They hoped to discover how people and cultures worked by studying them in what French sociologist Emile Durkheim called "their most elemental form." But just as scientists cannot tell everything about water by breaking it down into the elements of hydrogen and oxygen, what most anthropologists discovered was that every culture was rich and complex. Still, the root notion that we can see something of ourselves by looking at unfamiliar human cultures proved to have some merit. One thing we learn from looking at other cultures is that human beings in every culture work. In most cultures we see a close association between the work performed and the culture's needs. People fish and farm because they need to eat. People

weave so as to have clothes; they work wood, stone, and clay to fashion
dwellings. Even religion can be seen as a logical outgrowth of a need to
understand, and perhaps even control, human destiny.

Everybody works. Not everyone works outside the home; not everyone works for money. But everyone works. We have erred not in valuing
work, but rather in valuing only work done for money—and the more
money, the better. Often we continue to practice in our congregations
what Jesus decried 2,000 years ago—giving the best seats to the wealthy
instead of to the good.

How much better it would be to recognize everyone's work. Theologians have traditionally distinguished between serving God *per vocation*
and *in vocation*. Traditionally, the religious (members of religious orders)
served God by having a vocation (*in vocation*); that, is a special job to
do in God's world. Laity, meanwhile, were to serve God through their
vocations (*per vocation*). One's particular work did not matter so long
as the job needed to be done. With the Protestant Reformation, and
particularly with the thought of John Calvin, the idea of particular vocation was extended to the laity. A man might not just accidentally be a
baker, a miller, or a farmer, but rather be "called" to one of these professions. A woman might be called to be an artist, a homemaker, a poet.
Fulfilling one's calling became a high priority for those with this mentality about work.

Sadly, our usual notions of work are mundane compared to these
older religious ideas about vocation. In today's world, work is either utterly profane—just a job done to earn money—or downplayed for other
reasons. Even many religious leaders will minimize the importance of
work, lest people fall into the idea that they are really doing something
of significance. These leaders think that any praise for human activity
is praise taken away from God, who alone deserves it. I would argue
that in mixing categories they have led their followers astray. Opposing
works righteousness—the idea that you can work enough good in the
world to earn your salvation—is not the same as dismissing work. Indeed
when all well-done work is valued, work is religiously noble because it
is one thing human beings can do to express their gratitude by being co-
creators of their world with the God who gave the power to effect change
through work. It is when only the highly compensated kinds of work (or
certain kinds of especially sacrificial work such as the professional ministry) are singled out as valuable that the Protestant work ethic becomes
a kind of Protestant works righteousness.

Not all work is equally pleasing before God. It is fair to say that being a hired killer, or pursuing another line of work that contributes to human misery is not a form of gratitude toward God. Nevertheless, work is the fundamental building block of an economy. One way to redescribe and demystify the economy is to see it as "the work that everyone does and the way it all works together." As we build outward from work, broadly construed, to economy, we move toward greater abstraction, but not necessarily away from clarity about the purposes for which an economy exists. The economy is the place where good things can happen among people working together. This does not mean that good things *will* happen in the economy. Rather it means that the economy is a context, and indeed the *only* context, for human flourishing.

## The Saint's View of Economy

What view of an economy is consistent with the outlook of a generous saint? A broad view. Just as people growing in faith often discover that their conception of God is too small, so people trying to be giving and holy may discover that their view of an economy is too narrow. It is notable that our word for economy is derived from the Greek word *oikos*. The concept of economy, also translated as "household," was a prevalent one in Hellenistic times when the New Testament was written. The people living in Jesus' time had a strong sense of an economy, but in their version of the concept it was the household and not the individual that formed the basic social unit. As we know from reading the New Testament, people were even converted and baptized as members of households.

On a larger scale, the early Christians viewed the cosmos in household terms as well. In this they were like their counterparts in the Greco-Roman world: all the world was but an infinitely extended household. In this view, all of us have rooms, places, relations, and locations in that household. All of us are in this vast household together, and there is no escape from it. The Christians, like the Hebrews before them, operated within this worldview with one huge exception: they assigned the patronage of the *oikos* to God, and not to Caesar. Ultimately everything going on within the world—visible and invisible—was part of the great household of God.

Reading the New Testament within a household-economy perspective opens new insights into the Scriptures. The household of God is also not a bad place for contemporary Christians to start thinking about the economy and their role in it. Ponder these questions:

- Do we think God would be happy with what is going on in God's household? If not, how can we change it?
- In our roles as members of the household of God, are we doing useful tasks or superfluous tasks?
- Do the ways in which we value particular kinds of work accord with their significance in the household of God?
- Are events happening with which we are sure God is pleased? How can we do more of those works and support one another in doing them?

If our definition of economic activity becomes the work that gets done in the household of God, we are much freer to be generous in spirit and in fact than if we were operating under the mentality of scarcity. For surely there is enough to go around in our congregations and communities. Generosity provides the next challenge: how to share what we have, so that in pleasing God we benefit our neighbors and ourselves.

If Christians understood economic activity in more holistic ways, there would undoubtedly be some jobs Christians would choose not to do. The greater the sense one has of working within God's household, the less attractive it will seem to make violent movies, to trade in harmful substances, or to engage in shady marketing techniques. This idea bothers some people, as though somehow the world might fall apart if any aspect of the current marketplace were affected by religious or moral concerns. Far from being a problem, it could be a sign of health. A more considered marketplace might result in a marketplace more consistent with the faith.

But still some will object that the market reflects only the aggregated tastes and preferences of its participants. If child-care workers are paid so little, it is because their work is not valuable to us, or is so easy that anyone can do it. If we love expensive sports shoes but do not want to pay dearly for them, it is no wonder that they are made by child and convict labor in developing countries. The market, its defenders will argue, is morally neutral. It efficiently gives the people what they want.

For the most part, I agree with this assessment. Markets do give people what they want, or at least they give people who have money to spend what they want. (And in the United States, nearly all people, even the poorest, exercise some economic preferences.) But the major caveat of economics, "tastes and preferences remaining equal," is not to be lightly glossed over. We get what we want. But do we want the right things? Do we have the right "tastes and preferences," or ought they to change? At this point our faith and other sources of morality re-enter the picture. Our faith ought to shape our preferences and not the other way around. If a Christian's preferences for luxuries do not differ from those of a hedonist, how are we to know that the Christian's faith means anything? Unfortunately, even some of the most fervently Bible-believing people in our time appear to have utterly secular tastes and preferences. Their faith stops just short of their workplace, their wallets, and their wants.

I am not a sectarian. The sectarian believes that all of life outside his or her church is dark and evil. In this view, the world and therefore the world's economy cannot be redeemed; economy and world alike are but necessary evils. Many members of contemporary Christian congregations are semi-sectarians. They believe that, on the one hand, the church ought to have a larger influence in common life. On the other hand, they tend to believe that this development is unlikely ever to occur. And so, while not accepting the full sectarian viewpoint, they separate the church from the world and divide their faith from their participation in the economy. Consequently, they tend to believe that the faith may have something to say about how one spends one's money but not much about how a person makes a living. If it is a jungle out there, then no possibilities exist for transcending jungle-rule, and the church, the family, and other small-scale voluntary organizations become the exclusive sphere for moral action. Human beings can be moral in the private sphere, but the public, economic, working sphere has its own rules, and as pastors are often told, "You just wouldn't understand how it is in my work."

My own work is in the context of a theological seminary. As dean, I read the applications of each student applying for a degree program. I am struck by how often students applying for the Master of Divinity program (that course of study usually leading to the ordained ministry) articulate as their reason for coming to seminary the discovery that their work within the church is more satisfying than their previous secular employment. Not infrequently, these applicants describe their former

work as not merely unsatisfying but also morally compromising. I am of course glad that some of the people who find their way into the ordained ministry are going to find a deep satisfaction in their calling. But I am also disturbed that the professional ministry is seen, at least in part, as an escape from the real world and its pressures in favor of entry into a cloistered and sacred life.

Such applications make me sad for two reasons. First, ministry, properly understood, is not an escape from the problems other disciples of Christ face. But more significantly, I wonder about the logic behind the escapee's thinking. To whom does this would-be minister think he or she will be ministering? Are all laity morally suspect because they are implicated in the dirty job of making money and taking care of business? Clearly, I do not think so. Not all the honorable and important work in this world is done inside the church, and the minister who realizes this truth is in a far better position to help parishioners make their own contributions in the so-called secular arena.

## A Generous View of Work

Congregations that seek to cultivate holiness and generosity on the part of their members need to attend to the places where their members spend a large proportion of their lives. Work, broadly construed, is where we expend our time and energy. Considering what we do with those precious, God-given resources is soul-work. For the Christian, there should be no area of life from which God is thought to be missing. Therefore, the most important question that pastors can ask their people, or that people can ask one another, is "What do you do with your time?" It's not a question about a job, or a question only for the employed. Everyone "works" in a larger, more generous view of work and economy.

If, as English novelist D. H. Lawrence said, "Money is our collective madness," then the workaday world of the market economy is the altar of insane idolatry to which we are seduced. The work of the contemporary congregation is to help each member find a worthwhile place in the household of God and to relate that role to the putative economy in a way that avoids idolatry. This is a fine line to walk, for we must not worship our jobs and the objects wrought by our own hands. Yet it is through the work of our hands and hearts that we make contributions to

the created order that glorify God. What we "do" matters, for all we have to give as human beings is expressed in time, effort, and love.

To make work count without making it count for everything is best accomplished by remembering three concepts. First, God is at the center of our work. Second, because God is at the center, our definition of work must be a generous one. No one in the congregation can be permitted to say, "Oh, I don't work," and no one should be made to feel (as our society often makes people feel) that what one does with one's time is not significant. In the household of God, everyone is doing something. Even things that do not seem to us to be work have household significance. Children may be playing, and the person in the hospice may be accepting care for her suffering, and the gardener may be smelling the rose instead of raking, but it all has significance. Third, we must remember that it is our goal to reconcile ourselves to God, and not God to us. Therefore, work that really matters is what matters before God. Important, God-pleasing work may not pay well. That is our problem and not God's difficulty.

Our congregations can help in the reconciliation process by lifting up the "widow's mite" kinds of contributions of their members and by raising the questions that lead to constructive self-examination. Sometimes we can approach generosity directly. When Mrs. Gaudens has given 10,000 hours in cumulative volunteer service at the hospice, we can celebrate that achievement in the congregations. Then we can ask her to witness to what she has learned in her work in the alternative economy of God about life, the human spirit, endurance, faith, and grace. The only way for people to make generous choices is to recognize those choices when they see them. The best way for people to learn to recognize a generous choice is to hear from a person who has already been there that the choice was worthwhile.

Sometimes we cultivate generosity by enlarging the imagination. Pastors, in particular, have the privilege of holding out alternative religious visions on behalf of God. One way we might enlarge our theological visions of work is to probe the matter indirectly, the way Jesus did, by telling parables. Consider the following, a new parable for our time:

### The Parable of the Two Lawyers

A woman had two sons. Both grew up and became lawyers. As each son graduated from law school, she told him, "Be a good lawyer, but remember to keep a place for God in your heart. Son, be sure to practice your religion."

One son became a successful attorney. He worked 70 hours a week for the real-estate clients his firm attracted. He remembered what his mother had told him, and though he rarely found time for anything outside his work, he never missed Sunday worship and gave a tithe of his considerable income to his church. When asked, he would say he was very happy with his life.

The other son built a modest practice on small transactions between small people and on the resolution of their problems with the law. He rarely worked more than 40 hours a week. He remembered what his mother had told him and spent countless hours volunteering in soup kitchens, laboring at Habitat for Humanity construction sites, and teaching clients to read. His income and his church attendance were unremarkable. When asked, he would say he was very happy with his life.

Who do you think did as his mother wished?

In strange and wonderful ways, where we find ourselves often proves to be conditioned by where we think we are. When we think we are lost, we usually are. When we think we are at the mercy of an impersonal, uncaring economy, we probably are. But when we situate ourselves within a world where a generous God is head of the household, the possibilities for work, life, and caring are greatly improved.

## Exercises

### Personal Matters

One way of helping ourselves understand our personal economic participation in more desirable, more godly terms is to picture ourselves at the end of life having a conversation with God about how we chose to spend our lives, time, and money. How would your conversation go with God?

What would you say about the way you used your time? What would
you say about choices you made about the kind of jobs you accepted?
What would you say about the kind of person you were in those jobs?
Now think prospectively. How would you like that conversation to go?
What would you like to have people say about you when you are gone?
Chances are, no one will say how much money you made or left behind,
or how many hours you worked. But if you can find your place in the
household of God, people will not lack for something good to say.

**If Money Were No Object**

What would you do with your time if you didn't need to earn a living?
Most people would hope to have more leisure, so assume that you can
get as much of that as you could possibly want. What else would you do
with your time? Work with children? Paint? Build boats? Be a better
friend? Cook? Fix up poor people's homes? What would you do? Where
in your life can you do more of the work about which you have passion?

Spend some time alone thinking through your answers. Then to the
degree that you are ready, share them in a small-group setting where you
ought to be known. Only with the encouragement of fellow disciples
will we ever have the courage to become in part what we would be in
our dreams.

# CHAPTER 3

# *What Does the Lord Require?*

Congregations sustain the faith and the faithful. Generous saints are raised up and supported in countless churches across the globe. In these churches, people gather and catch a vision of what God intends for human life. In these congregations, people are reminded that their worth far exceeds their money and that their primary economic role is as a member of the household of God. Already we have seen some of the characteristic ways that Christian congregations behave. On the other hand, congregations come in myriad shapes and sizes, and we live in a time when many are experiencing formidable challenges to sustaining the way they have operated for more than a generation. Times like these cause us to ask questions: Are there any commonalities among congregations, any bottom lines, any essentials? What is a congregation and what does it need to do its work? Or, to put the congregational-identity question theologically: What does the Lord require of the people who gather in God's name?

## What Every Church Needs

It was a hot summer presbytery meeting in Ann Arbor, in 1981. I had returned to the Detroit Presbytery from seminary in the East, hoping to do my part in an urban-ministry internship. Youthful enthusiasm and a commitment to the church in the city fueled my interest in the next item on the docket. The agenda said we would be discussing a "white paper" on the future of the presbytery. Great, I thought; someone is engaging in some forward thinking about how to reverse the negative mood of the church in this metropolitan area. In the years since the race riots of

1968, Detroit had fallen on hard times, and even the churches that had sought to stay were hard-pressed to keep body and soul together.

It turned out, however, that this so-called white paper was prepared by the pastor of a large-membership suburban congregation, who sought to persuade his fellow presbyters to "face the facts" as he saw them. Nearly 20 years later, the rhetorical flavor sticks with me. The litany of "facts" that opened the exposé went something like this:

*Fact:* To be viable, a church needs, at minimum, a full-time minister, a full-time secretary, and a full-time janitor, together with a part-time choir director and a part-time organist. The cost of this minimal personnel is $50,000.

*Fact:* The cost of insurance, utilities, and printing raises the total cost of just opening the doors of a church for business to $70,000.

*Fact:* The average pledge per member in the United Presbyterian Church is $280.00 per year.

*Fact:* Given the cost of keeping a church open and the average size of pledges in the Presbyterian Church, the minimum number of members for a sustainable church is 250.

The exposé next turned from these incontrovertible facts to implications for the future. The presbytery's job, as the author saw it, was to figure out how to close weak churches before they took down the strong ones (like his) with them in a lifeboat overloaded with misplaced compassion. My initial appetite for the discussion turned to a serious case of sour stomach. What in the world did killing off the weak have to do with being the Christian church?

I observe several ironies when I think back on that time. The first of these is that the mean size of Presbyterian Church (USA) congregations is now below the 250 mark then depicted as minimally viable. Another is that some churches consigned to abandonment in the white paper survived, while some churches that then had 500 members have long since failed.

I would like to think that what I experienced on that summer day was a bad moment never since repeated elsewhere in the North American

church. What I find, on the contrary, is that this kind of thinking about viability and the needed resources for being a congregation is pervasive.

What is so awful about this approach is that it is not Christian. The only biblical requirement we have for the minimum size of Christian congregations is Christ's promise that "where two or three are gathered in my name, I am there among them" (Matt. 18:20). That's pretty minimal, isn't it? Other marks of the true church from Christian history typically focus on such matters as the church being the place where the word of God is rightly preached and the sacraments rightly celebrated.

In many ways the contemporary American church's crisis is not about financing our congregations, but rather about continuing to afford a style of church to which we have become accustomed.

I received a real education the year of that memorable presbytery meeting, because I went straight from an urban ministry internship to a solo pastoral charge in New York's Catskill Mountains, where the attitude toward viability could not have been more different from that prevailing in Detroit.

New York state west of the Hudson River is often in church history called the "burned-over district." Early in the 1800s the revival flames of the Second Great Awakening burned bright indeed. Every pioneer or tannery settlement experienced the Awakening, and a church or two or more was left behind. When I arrived in the Catskills, between waning ardor for the Gospel and shifts in population and economy, the churches left behind by the revivals had been declining for almost 170 years. But while the metro Detroit pastors thought about closing down small-membership churches, the Methodist, Baptist, Presbyterian, Episcopal, and Roman Catholic churches that dotted the Catskills had largely given up the idea that closing churches solved anything.

Rather they were asking the question of viability from a different starting point. They recognized that their churches had limited potential for growth, dispersed as they were in small villages. They had seen that closing the church in one village and telling its members to worship in the next town over, eight miles away, was futile. But they also saw that their churches, in the main, were not getting smaller and that they were meeting the spiritual and religious needs of people living in these country areas to be the people of God in a particular place. In other words, the leaders of the region saw that their churches were spiritually viable and that their problem was how to reorganize structurally so that what

was spiritually viable could be sustained financially. A wide variety of solutions was employed: student ministers learned by experience; retired ministers served pastorates in exchange for housing and a small stipend; college religion professors and hospital chaplains preached part-time; congregations sponsored the theological training of their own members as lay ministers; some churches shared a full-time minister. Viability had a new meaning, and I was getting a two-part education in practical ecclesiology.

## The Measure of Our Success

Abraham Lincoln once said that he had found that people are about as happy as they make up their minds to be. A similar form of self-constructive work happens with religious institutions. Churches can be only as successful as they are allowed to be by the terms for success they have set for themselves. It is possible to enter a sanctuary with 250 worshipers on a Sunday morning and to catch a vibrant sense of that congregation's joy in being together. It is also possible to walk into a service in another church where 500 people are gathered and have a sense that all present know that something is missing. Clearly the difference is not in the absolute levels of participation; otherwise everyone would say that the church with 500 worshipers was twice as successful. Often feelings of success come with numerical growth, so that the church with 250 worshipers may be glorying in the fact that last year there would have been only 220 people present on a Sunday morning. Likewise, the members of the church with 500 worshipers may be asking themselves why they don't have 650 worshipers as they did five years earlier. Often feelings of success and failure are tied to numbers. And growth or decline in the numbers of congregational adherents correlates closely with the financial wherewithal to carry out the congregation's program. But blaming a decrease in numbers for a congregation's feelings of failure is like blaming one's temperature for one's flu symptoms. In each case numbers— whether they measure temperature or worship attendance—are an indicator and not an underlying cause of health or illness.

Trying to keep up with the most numerically and financially successful churches can doom a congregation to dissatisfaction. In Lincoln's terms, it's making up the collective mind to be unhappy unless by external measures we excel all our neighbors. A congregation preordains

itself to disappointment also by comparing the present church to its former glory—to the days when the preaching was better, the Sunday school was bursting at the seams, and the flower chart in the narthex was fully subscribed for the coming year on the first day it was posted. The church of today can rarely compete with the memories of its glorious past, particularly a past remembered with retrospective glory brighter than that which existed in reality.

The question of how religious people are to judge their actions and institutions is as old as the Scriptures themselves. The question is posed in many ways in the tradition. Some ask, "What must I do to be saved?" Others inquire, "What will make God happy?" One of the most enduring and forceful expressions of this question is "What does the Lord require?" It is a question that we usually try to answer individually but one that needs also to be asked of the body of believers. It is notable that in the two places in the Bible where we find a summary of what the Lord God requires, the requirements are directed not to individuals but to a collective people. In Deuteronomy 10, the essence of the Law is presented this way:

> So now, O Israel, what does the LORD your God require of you? Only to fear the LORD your God, to walk in all his ways, to love him, to serve the LORD your God with all your heart and with all your soul, and to keep the commandments of the LORD your God and his decrees that I am commanding you today, for your own well-being. (Deut. 10:12-13).

In Deuteronomy, obedience to Yahweh's requirements cannot be pursued alone, but only through the people of Israel. The Hebrew people cannot be rewarded for their obedience as isolated individuals, but only as a people with collective prospects. Can such hope be sustained? Of course, say the Scriptures, for by fearing and worshiping Yahweh alone, the people will know that their God "is your praise; he is your God, who has done for you these great and awesome things that your own eyes have seen. Your ancestors went down to Egypt seventy persons; and now the LORD your God has made you as numerous as the stars in heaven" (Deut. 10:21-22).

In Micah, the requirements of justice, love, and humility are juxtaposed with the anxious individualism of the sacrificial system. Things

are going badly. "What can I do?" is the question of the hour. Can I make things right with God by means of burnt offerings? How about lots of burnt offerings? A thousand rams? Ten thousand rivers of oil, or even my firstborn? No, says Micah, it is at the same time simpler and harder:

> He has told you, O mortal, what is good;
> and what does the LORD require of you
> but to do justice, and to love kindness,
> and to walk humbly with your God? (Mic. 6:8).

To do justice requires relationships with other human beings. It is impossible to fulfill Yahweh's command in isolation. To love kindness requires that the soul turn outward. To walk humbly means to subsume one's own purposes and the group's purposes to those of God. Once again, the Bible reminds us that we do not own ourselves. And so what of our churches? Are they not even more the possession of God and not of ourselves? The passage in Micah that states the admonition to justice, kindness, and humility is followed immediately by a stern cry from the prophet in the voice of Yahweh to the "assembly of the city." Those who follow the deceitful desires of their own hearts can have what they want, but it will not satisfy:

> You shall eat, but not be satisfied,
>     and there shall be a gnawing hunger within you;
> you shall put away, but not save,
>     and what you save, I will hand over to the sword.
> You shall sow, but not reap;
>     you shall tread olives, but not anoint yourselves with oil;
> you shall tread grapes, but not drink wine (Mic. 6:14-15).

If there is a lesson for the contemporary church, it is this: that our busyness in today's congregations is not the same thing as *being* the church. Even if our tendency to become absorbed in church activities is not outright deceit, it is more like the burnt-offerings game than it is the work of the people of God in relationship to their God. Jesus knew how many people preferred *looking* religious to *being* religious. In the Sermon on the Mount he said, "And whenever you fast, do not look dismal, like the hypocrites, for they disfigure their faces so as to show others

that they are fasting. Truly I tell you, they have received their reward"
(Matt. 6:16). If we wonder why our church life fails to satisfy, despite
all our programs, buildings, organs, and services, perhaps we are missing
something more fundamental, something more closely related to the purposes of God.

When Jesus was asked to summarize his understanding of what God
requires by citing the greatest commandment, he replied: "'You shall
love the Lord your God with all your heart, and with all your soul, and
with all your mind.' This is the greatest and first commandment. And a
second is like it: 'You shall love your neighbor as yourself.' On these
two commandments hang all the law and the prophets" (Matt. 22:37-
40). If that is what we are to do, then what is the church to do and be?
American theologian H. Richard Niebuhr answered that the purpose of
the church's ministry is the increase in knowledge and love of God and
love toward neighbor.

So a church is where two or more are gathered in the name of
Christ, where the love of God is advanced, and where love for neighbor
is increased. What the Lord requires is a much simpler basis for forming
a church than what most of us think possible, but it is a liberating definition because most gatherings of Christians could—by these standards—
be successful.

## A Sense of Direction

Let us return to those worshiping congregations numbering 250 and 500.
While it may be that one is on the way up and the other on the way
down, it is more likely that the root cause of the joy in the one (and of
the lamentation in the other) is the joyful congregation's sense of what
it is doing, whose it is, and how that fits what the Lord requires. What
the Lord requires of a church is very little from the standpoint of absolute resources, but it includes a commitment to orient the use of those
resources absolutely to the fundamental and important purpose of being
God's people of justice, kindness, humility, praise, and love.

Meanwhile, it is likely that the sad congregation has lost its way.
Congregations falter when they confuse the trappings of church with its
mission, and when they mistake a great past history with the purpose of
their journey. When a congregation can fondly remember where it has

been but does not see itself still journeying toward God, it has lost the nourishment it needs to sustain life. Just as people in poor health who have lost a sense of purpose lose also the will to live and often have difficulty sustaining life by eating and drinking, so too a congregation that has lost a sense of forward movement and purpose will have trouble sustaining its body with an inflow of money and new members. A memorial to past experience is a poor substitute for current religious experience. A memorial can only partially hold the attention of those who recall the experience. It cannot attract those who never had a taste of the real. Who wants to join a church that has memory but no hope? The saddest of all losing propositions is "This was a great church and could be again with some new members."

There are other diagnostic clues to suggest that a congregation is missing its sense of direction. Some congregations collectively grieve the loss of what they had before. The loss may be members, but it may also be neighborhood safety, or even members' own youthfulness. Many congregations founded 40 to 50 years ago succeeded in their task as suburban pioneers, but they are having trouble ceding power to a new generation. It is as if only the founding generation can be faithful, and once a church is built and sustained there is nowhere to go. Congregations may exhibit jealousy toward what other congregations have. A family-life center does not make a vital congregation any more than having 250 members, but many congregations without such a facility are fixated on getting one as a panacea for all their problems.

A final diagnostic marker for congregational disorientation is an excess of blame. All over the United States we find people in churches blaming pastors, lay leaders, even congregational events for things beyond a congregation's control. Neighborhoods do change. They age, mature, and turn over to new demographic groups. Youth grow up and leave the youth group for college and work; often they move away. Congregation members who are generous givers near the end of their lives die and are replaced by less generous, younger, sometimes struggling members. All of these transitions are predictable facts of life, largely outside a pastor's or congregation's control. Yet a congregation that does not have a positive, hopeful sense of being God's people and of having both a home and things to do no matter what befalls it can spend years blaming its leaders for failing in the hopeless task of making what was once gold stay.

Many churches are, I believe, living on borrowed time. They are still moving, but their movement masks the fact that their clergy and lay leaders have no idea where they are going, theologically speaking. There are still other churches where things are going right, where God is served and neighbors are loved, but where the congregation's leaders and members are not especially clear *why* things are going well. Most congregations can benefit from examining how the spiritual requirements of being the church might influence the institutional choices we make. To put it directly, the way we "do church" ought to be a direct outgrowth of where we believe God wants us to go.

## The Road Ahead

Congregations need a sense of direction, but not just any direction. They need to orient themselves in God's direction. We have strong general convictions and intuitions from the tradition itself about what God desires of the church. As we have indicated, the church is directed in every time and place toward love of God and neighbor and, as such, is in constant pursuit of justice, kindness, and humility before God. What worked 25 years ago, however, may not be the way a congregation lives out those directions today. The forms that today's congregations take ought to be both a reflection of the church's perennial purposes and the specific challenges of our current and future situation.

The very word "disorientation" has a Christian origin. It comes from the ancient practice of situating the head, or altar end, of a cruciform church toward the East. Unlike other religious groups that rely upon a sacred point fixed in space (as for example Muslims with their Mecca), Christians "oriented" their churches to the East in recognition of the Easter event, the fresh dawn of new life in the resurrected Christ. A disoriented church, therefore, is a church that has lost its sense of which way is east. More important, a disoriented church has lost its sense of the place of the Easter event in its community.

When it comes to helping disoriented congregations reclaim their way, I find a great deal of insight in some contemporary writing about the church. Indeed, I think Christians today are on the leading edge of a movement in ecclesiology—a making sense of the church—that gives us strong material out of which to reorient our congregations.

Several of the guides to reorienting the church concentrate on the practices congregations use in their shared lives. For theologian Letty Russell, the metaphor of the round table serves as an apt vision for what today's church should look like. No one can be at the head of a round table. The mutuality of voices, identities, and people in the church is to be stressed. For another theologian, Lewis S. Mudge, ecclesiology ought to emerge out of a faithful people's self-understanding. A church with a prospect of a future is shaped around a contemporary "sense of a people," not around a centuries-old blueprint.

Robert Wuthnow is a sociologist and not a theologian of the church. Still, in several books he and his colleagues have probed the human groups and experiences that give life meaning and purpose. In studying small groups in particular, he has found them to be potent transformative contexts for people of faith. In his research small groups almost always proved to be the most salient (literally, salty) experience in their members' lives. Yet Wuthnow mentioned to me in correspondence that he could not find an example of a small group that had lasted more than 30 years. Why would they last when 20 percent of the U.S. population moves each year? Indeed, very few small groups make it beyond a decade. But congregations do last, because they are formed with member replacement and survival in mind.

One conclusion that can be drawn from Wuthnow's work is that churches need to find ways to be stable, ongoing congregational contexts for the small groups that rise and fall and touch and change people's lives. In fact, small groups serve needs so effectively that it would be tempting to try to make a congregation simply a holding company for small groups. People could then feel comfortable, or better, or even challenged. But congregations at their best are more than the sum of their parts. Most important, they can serve as a bulwark against an unwarranted domestication of the Gospel. That is, they remind us that the Gospel is there not just to meet our need for nurture. And yet, if this people-nurturing aspect of the church's life is neglected, then we will surely have no church. Our churches must be both a "Balm in Corporateland" and a foretaste of how things might be different.

Loren Mead argued in *The Once and Future Church* (Bethesda, Md.: The Alban Institute, 1991) that real transformation of the church would come from a broad-based movement of theological education of the laity, not from more or better-trained clergy who kept the secrets of

the Kingdom to themselves. A collective of theologians and church leaders called the Gospel and Our Culture Network, led by George Hunsberger and others, has produced one of the most telling ecclesiological programs. In a book titled *Missional Church* (ed. Darrell L. Guder, Grand Rapids, Mich.: William B. Eerdmans, 1998) these authors argue that the most basic form of the church is the congregation and that the church at this level above all others must have an experience of itself being sent by God into the world to work and witness. By contrast, most congregations in North America are trapped in serving as chaplains to their culture. It is in the concept of the missional church, I would argue, that some of the many themes of contemporary ecclesiological discussion come together. The missional congregation is called to be

1. Not pastor-centered, but inclusive of the whole people of God.
2. Gospel-motivated instead of culturally captive.
3. Complex enough to be stable as a congregation and flexible enough to sponsor the small groups and *ecclesioli* (little churches inside the church) through which personal transformation really takes place.
4. Theologically aware of whose it is.
5. Articulate about its mission with programs that match its orientation.

Finally, the emerging healthy and missional congregation is one that knows that there is no single model for a Christian congregation. It is confident enough that other groups' religious lifestyles and programs do not undermine its sense of mission. That confidence extends even to the congregations of other religious faiths. This new model of being a healthy congregation in a pluralistic world is one that witnesses to its positive anthropology (its constructive account of what people are all about) with the expectation that the religious value system of any other functioning culture will be able to do the same. In letters to the young churches of the New Testament period, the writer of the Johannine epistles urged congregations to demonstrate their faith by love. At the beginning of the third millennium, the old business of "see how they love one another" is precisely the new business of witness in the post-Christendom world.

# Lifestyle Changes for the Missional Church

Rethinking the institutional requirements of being the church for people who struggle to be faithful members of God's household in the 21st century is not unlike deciding on lifestyle changes when facing a major life transition like marriage, the birth of a child, or retirement. For both individuals and the church, one of the most obvious places to start is the question, "Where shall we live?" At some points in life, people find themselves needing more space than they have. On the other hand, retirees often find themselves in homes that are too large and more suited to family-rearing than to their current needs. They may also find that the upkeep requirements of their dwellings are more than they wish to meet, financially or physically. It is not unusual, therefore, for a retired individual or couple to make a major move down in size of home.

In like manner, many of today's congregations find themselves living in split-level church homes that no longer fit their collective lifestyles. This is true whether congregational change is numerically up or down. But to a much greater degree than with individual housing choices, the congregation has a tendency to hold on to its home long after its needs have changed. A large part of this insistence has to do with the sentimentality that attaches to place and the high social costs that come with starting over. The very widow who gladly exchanges a three-bedroom tract home for a new condominium may wish to retain some sense of personal historical continuity through her church.

As a result of all the collective forces at work, we get a situation in which congregations are overinvested in property in particular locations. At one level this investment is a strength. Congregations do not desert neighborhoods the way drugstores, film developers, and fast-food outlets do. Persistence in place is often a virtue in a market- and change-driven society. However, when churches become servants to their property, what was a strength often becomes a liability. Churches are then implicated in a pathology sometimes called the "edifice complex." Since so much organizational effort and financial resources are tied up in maintaining a physical presence in a particular place, one of the key things every congregation needs to ask itself is whether its home suits its mission now and whether it will continue to do so for the foreseeable future.

People often make other lifestyle changes at retirement. They stop taking the newspaper, or they start taking the paper and actually reading

it. They walk more; they volunteer more time to their favorite causes. Retirement would be hell if it meant simply doing exactly the same things except not going to work. Most people don't live that way, and the church can learn from the human experience of members who know that retirement is not submission in defeat but a chance to do more and different kinds of living. Indeed, just as the best-adjusted individuals accept life changes as personal opportunities, congregations facing challenges to longtime ways of operating ought to view those challenges as an opportunity to break with the past and get on with more exciting tasks than propping up an unsustainable lifestyle. With this aim in mind, here are 20 steps that congregations might take to lessen the grip of financial exigency and enhance their missional vitality.

## Church Lifestyle Change Ideas for Generous Saints

- Buy a smaller building to reduce upkeep and overhead.
- Relocate to a site more in keeping with your mission.
- Use less of your building. Wall off portions that are used poorly but still require heat.
- Share a building with an immigrant or ethnic congregation.
- Develop commercial or not-for-profit office space in your building, and let it pay for your fixed costs so that giving can go to missions.
- Invent a new ministry that emerges out of your congregation's rediscovery of its context.
- Hold a Bible school for adults with the same generosity of spirit you would display toward neighborhood children. That is, don't do it because you need the members. (Everybody can spot desperation.) Do it because everybody needs the Gospel.
- Revise your definition of what clergy and laity do. Use more laypeople to engage in frontline ministry; use clergy to train the new lay ministers.
- Don't worry about whether the clients of a hosted ministry will or won't join your church. Worry instead about whether you are making an adequate witness to your faith through that ministry. Ask yourselves: Are our members who volunteer for the ministry fulfilled?
- Meet for spiritual purposes in small groups in homes without the expectation that clergy will be present. Ministry is too vital to wait for an ordained minister.

- During periods of extreme heat or cold, share services with a neighboring church, both to save on utilities and to witness to your common bonds in Christ.
- Downsize the bureaucracy. Eliminate unnecessary offices and board positions, but increase opportunities for direct, meaningful, and well-supported lay ministry.
- Decrease the number of mailings, but increase their impact. Use less staff-produced material and more firsthand accounts from members about their faith and experiences.
- Share the cleaning of the church and grounds to free money for mission; hire more of the cleaning out if you can use members' time to even better purpose.
- Re-evaluate fund-raisers. Are you burnt out as a group? Do fund-raising activities increase your group energy and commitment or sap it? Would you rather do direct service? What do your publicly visible activities tell your neighbors about the God you worship?
- During the summer, when air conditioning is not needed for health reasons, bring out the fans, turn down the lights, and donate the difference to a need that really matters. Say it out loud—we'd rather give that money away to our friends in Haiti!
- Stop reinventing the wheel. When someone suggests reorganizing the church committee structure, ask first whether you are going to do something different or just do the same things differently as a result of your efforts.
- Carry out activities in parallel small groups. For example, try Bible reading. Every member of the congregation is spending three months reading Paul's letter to the Romans, but each is doing this in a small group.
- Worship outside your walls once in a while to remind yourselves that a religious congregation is a people and not a building.
- Rediscover the significance of community by talking to neighbors outside the church. Talk about what you learn. Let your consciences guide your next moves.

There are no moves that are right for every congregation. It matters not so much whether you tear down the gym to make room for a senior center or build a gym for the first time. What matters is whether the action taken is fitting to the congregation's mission. To be vital, what the

congregation most needs is a sense of direction. A church on the move is rarely tempted to look backward. Why? Because it has a sense of the future—a hopeful sense that God is not done with it yet.

Rethinking congregational lifestyles with God's requirements in mind is more like planning for a journey than like building a fortress we hope will last forever. Consider the questions we ask when we plan a journey: Where do we want to go? What supplies do we need? What needs must be cared for to make the journey possible for our companions? What do we have to leave behind to move forward? How do we make that leaving possible? Congregations facing change need to ponder two facts: No one can build a church that is guaranteed to thrive 100 years from now, yet everyone can journey with God.

# Exercise

### Burning Down the Church

One way for us as members of congregations to rethink the institutional requirements of being the church in our way and in our day is to get outside the framework of thinking about our church as a building in a given location. For the purpose of discussion, let's assume that a tragic fire has destroyed our church building. It is up to us to decide what we ought to do with the insurance settlement. Let's discuss the following questions:

- Are we called to be a congregation?
- Do we need a building to be faithful to our call?
- Should we rebuild in the same location? Why or why not?
- What features about our congregation's mission do we especially value?
- What kind of building and program will we construct, since we have to start afresh? What are the implications for personnel, space, and budget?
- Are there new opportunities for mission God is calling us to undertake since we are free to start over?

After spending enough time on the exercise to allow all members present to be heard and to hear one another, identify common themes from the discussion and place these themes on newsprint or a blackboard. Next discuss two final questions:

* Are there things we have learned about ourselves by imagining that we had to rebuild—things that reflect our aspirations and goals for this congregation?
* In the absence of a fire, what can we do to structure our congregation more nearly as we think God would have us do now?

# CHAPTER 4

# *Financing a Congregation of Saints*

One perennial problem of the Christian congregation is how to collect the resources required to pursue its mission. From the early churches reported in the book of Acts to the present, the followers of Christ have needed to collect and disburse money. Perhaps we can trace the practice of church finance even further back to the time of Jesus, when Judas acted as treasurer for the common purse of Jesus' group of disciples. For nearly 2,000 years, then, organized Christianity has coexisted with economies that use money as a medium of exchange. One might think that given this long history of having to finance their churches, Christians would have developed adequate systems of finance. To the contrary, American churches at the close of the 20th century find themselves with a tenuous grasp on the resources needed to pay for the ministries in which they are engaged.

The most common term used to denote the raising of funds in American Protestant churches during the past 100 years is "stewardship," a word also recently embraced by the Roman Catholic Church in the United States, as well as by environmentalists and others outside the church. It is a term full of promise—that somehow there will be enough to go around, that husbanded resources will multiply, and that taking the high road will result in maximum funds with minimum sacrifice. Nevertheless, a review of most contemporary attempts to carry out stewardship programs leads to the conclusion that most of these efforts are failures. Contemporary stewardship falls flat for one of two reasons. In the first instance funds are raised, but they are raised through the use of fun and games, through manipulation of members, through motivations based on guilt rather than grace, and through the embrace of a whole host of historical fictions about how much more faithful one's forebears in the

faith were than one's own generation. So in the first case, the money is raised, but the church relinquishes something of its character in the process. Pastors especially ought to be careful about using some of the contemporary methods for raising funds in the local church, lest they find themselves preaching one Gospel from the pulpit on Sunday morning and another through the actions of the church when the time comes to pay the piper.

Ironically, the second way the practice of contemporary stewardship usually fails is by churches' applying the theology of stewardship to all phases of life *except* money. Thus books have been written and sermons preached about how stewardship means care for the environment, for our brothers and sisters, for the children of the planet, and even for the structures of government. Yet when it comes to money, many of these books and sermons are squeamish. These authors and preachers have taken the high road and discussed in theologically sophisticated terms God's gift to human beings of dominion over creation. But consideration of money, the use of money, and particularly the giving of money to advance the work of the church is often absent (with the possible exception of money given for overseas missions). When included, the topic of money is rarely presented with the same degree of care as matters related to, say, environmentalism. Yet again, pastors can find themselves undermining their preaching and teaching ministries by suggesting that stewardship applies to everything except the only thing most laypeople thought it meant in the first place—supporting the church financially.

This chapter suggests how congregations and their pastors might get beyond these two sticking places in contemporary congregational finance and move toward raising the needed financial resources with theological integrity. Before moving to the constructive task of building a sound approach, we need to understand in greater detail what is wrong with most of the popular approaches in our churches today to raising funds and promoting stewardship.

## Fun and Games, Guilt and Shame

The most popular approaches to "painless" church fund-raising employ gimmicks designed to rope people into giving, and specifically giving

more to the church. One popular program, Pony Express, works by breaking the congregation down into small numbers of pledging units listed in order underneath the "trail boss." In the weeks leading up to the campaign, church leaders stress the importance of getting one's saddle-bag through, and making the decision to put one's pledge in the saddle-bag and move it along to the next family as soon as possible. As with a chain letter, one must not break the continuity, or one's peers are let down. Pony Express is so popular that it has spawned a variety of imi-tators, including the United Methodist Publishing House's Circuit Rider version. In each case these programs work by achieving high levels of donor participation. Church members are asked to think prayerfully about their pledges, but more than that, they are reminded of the impor-tance of getting the Pony Express mail through.

So what's wrong with a little fun and games? Don't people some-times need a little extra incentive to do the right thing? Well, if the old system had its faults—raising church funds by inducing guilt from the pulpit to goad members into contributing something approaching a tithe—so too do the rapid, serial-participation plans involve a degree of psychological manipulation. Here, instead of guilt, the motivating force is shame. One dare not fail one's peers. One must get the saddlebag through. More than that, despite words voiced to the contrary, it would be shameful not to add one's own envelope to the "saddlebag."

These popular systems for raising money in the church have their antecedent in the subscription-book system used by voluntary organiza-tions in the first half of the 19th century. There, however, a system of shame and praise was even more central. One's name and the amount pledged would be listed on one line of the subscription book; the book would be carried to the next member of the voluntary organization, who would likewise write in his or her name and the amount pledged. The key to raising funds under that system was to have gifts generous in proportion to the means of the givers listed early on in the subscription book. A small gift from a wealthy person or a piddling gift from any donor tended to attract similar levels of giving from subsequent donors. The important thing to notice about both the open-book and saddlebag versions of making the rounds with a pledging book is that there is nothing necessarily religious about one's giving under these systems. The motivations have to do with maintaining face in the eyes of others.

Another common fun-and-games way to raise money in contempo-rary churches is the venerable thermometer bar graph, filled in week by

week as people complete their pledges toward a predefined goal. There the sanctions are not so obviously negative. Instead, the playful device communicates that every pledge makes a positive contribution toward the church's finances. Church members may also be encouraged to take away a puzzle piece that will be returned with their completed pledge forms to make a reconstructed picture of the church that represents everyone doing his or her bit. Fellowship fund-raising is also a common practice in American churches. Be the vehicle a dinner, a show, or an auction, the purpose is the same: to have a little fun and fellowship and to create value that others will willingly exchange for cash to raise money for the church.

Such activities are to be honored for their ability to help create friendship within the fellowship, but the ethicist Gibson Winter's critique of this kind of activity nearly 40 years ago still rings true. He argued that any system in which people gladly perform menial chores they would just as soon avoid at home, and then gladly pay extra for the leftovers, probably represented a peculiarly Protestant form of penance. Once again, these fund-raising practices deserve theological scrutiny, for they may be effective in raising money for all the wrong reasons. Does this mean that all church fund-raisers and lighthearted attempts to encourage pledging are to be eschewed? No, but a fundamental awareness of why one ought to give to the church may result in a reduced reliance upon gimmicks.

Two of the more interesting and less problematic fund-raising practices are the every-member canvass and a process commonly known as "rating the prospects." The every-member canvass is labor-intensive, requiring teams of two or three church members to make calls on their fellow members. Callers bring a pledge card, stress the reasons for making an income-proportional or increased commitment to the church, and facilitate their church members' participation in the financial support of the church. The every-member canvass, as traditionally practiced, is less common than it was 40 years ago, in part because it has become increasingly difficult to find even committed Christians at home on a Sunday afternoon. Residual Sabbath-keeping instincts have largely given way to recreational pursuits. Thus, the every-member canvass has become logistically more difficult. But even if people could be found at home, the canvass is often disliked by people who resist being cast in the role of sales agent. Without a willingness on the part of callers to

attest personally to the benefits of giving to the mission of the church, the every-member canvass dissolves into an almost pointless exercise of mail delivery by inefficient means.

The process known as "rating the prospects" is relatively uncommon in Protestant and Catholic churches except when they are attempting major capital campaigns. This approach is much more common in religious-based and other philanthropic federated movements. A group of leaders committed to the values of the organization, having proved their commitment through a high degree of generosity, and having been chosen for their knowledge of the community, sit down together and evaluate what a "fair share" contribution might be from other donors known to them. They calculate the "fair share" on the basis of knowledge and assumptions about prospective donors' incomes and assets. Once the prospective donors are rated, they are approached by campaign leaders and told in effect, we are making this kind of pledge, and we believe you are in a position to make that kind of pledge if you too are committed to the purposes of this organization.

This type of fund-raising tends to be highly effective, but it does not lend itself to the contemporary practice of drawing church leaders from all ages and walks of life. It relies upon givers who are exemplary or socially elite reaching out to peers and those who would be their peers. What makes it an interesting form of fund-raising for churches is that it, like the every-member canvass, provides an opening for people seeking funds to witness to the value they experience in giving to the mission of the institution. Nevertheless, it is still possible to conduct a successful campaign by this means solely on the basis of saving face with community elites.

## Historical Fictions

When people are not trying to raise money for their churches by following the perfect technique, they can often be found promoting historical fictions about how money "always" used to be raised and given. The strongest of these myths goes something like this: "Back in the 19th century everyone (at least in Protestant churches) tithed." The truth of the matter is somewhat different. Tithing was actually a recovered practice, cloaked in a biblical precedent by the same people who claimed

that the wine present at the Last Supper came from unfermented grapes. These 19th-century eisegetes happened upon using the Davidic monarchy's short-lived financing scheme only after the town-finance, subscription-book, and pew-rental methods of raising church funds each failed to produce enough revenue. Preaching the tithe may have produced more income, yet apart from the Mormons, no major religious group in American history has ever succeeded in getting its members to give anything close to one-tenth of their incomes.

Convenient fictions, however, die slow deaths. We ought to ask why. In this case, the driving factor is perhaps the fear of what will happen if religious leaders give up the right to command 10 percent of their members' resources through guilt. Recent studies suggest that a range of 2.5 percent to 4 percent of income is a more typical giving range among Protestants, with a somewhat lower range for Catholics. In any case, mainline groups that have equivocated on the interpretation of biblical Scripture in matters related to gender relations, sexuality, and science often place themselves in a curious position when they defend tithing as a "biblical practice" in the face of massive defection by otherwise faithful members, who choose not to tithe.

Another powerful historical myth about the church that persists as if it were passed down with the Gospel is that there is only one way to support mission. No topic is likely to draw more heat from denominational stewardship experts than the desire of congregations and individuals to designate their gifts for particular causes. One hears statements like "The designated-giving movement represents a complete rejection of the Christian stewardship movement." Examining the history of fund-raising for religious causes, and for charitable causes more broadly, one finds different ethics at different times that present themselves as the "most Christian way to do things." Unified giving, the alternative to the "designated giving" dismissed in the myth, is simply the most recent successful claimant to the title of "most Christian way to do things."

The most important thing to emerge from insight into the ebb and flow of "Christian" ways to raise money is that unified approaches to religious finance are highly dependent upon social consensus. By contrast, periods with high levels of social change appear to lead to the formation of new causes, which must take their need for funds directly to potential givers, either as individuals or as churches. Such was the case during the Antebellum and Social Gospel eras with their respective

attempts to reform society. Likewise, rapid social change is probably the source of the proliferation of new charities making direct appeals since 1980 based on concern for homelessness, AIDS, international globalization, and increasing income disparity. Other periods, such as the 1910s and 1920s and 1945-1960, were times of significant trust in large-scale institutions like denominations and charitable federations to carry on efficiently the agreed-upon social agenda emerging from the previous generation of religious-social involvement. The theological overlay of this "we used to be united" myth serves mostly to obscure the level of social disagreement among contemporary Christians.

## Reclaiming Stewardship

Stewardship as a theological concept is cheapened when we use it as an exact synonym for financing the local church. Even expanding our definition of stewardship to include time and talent as well as treasure given to the church domesticates stewardship to merely its church resource-gathering dimension. If we are going to use the word stewardship around the church, we must be sure to liberate it from the narrow connotations we have given it over the years. Much as women's liberation was about seeing women as more than wives and mothers, we need to see stewardship as more than church fund-raising and the management of volunteers.

So what is stewardship, properly understood? Stewardship is the responsive practice of human beings tending to what has been placed in their care by God. It is a responsive practice in the sense that it is something people do because God has first done something to and for them. Stewardship is the peculiar response that human beings can make to the Creator who has both blessed them with gifts and ceded dominion over the creation.

Dominion is often understood to justify whatever human beings want to do with their world, their environment, and other creatures. But rooted in the text of Genesis we find the true meaning of God's entrusting act. Entrusting creation to the human creature in a way different from all others was not God's way of saying, "Here's the world; do whatever you want with it." Rather, the meaning of the act was to say, in effect, "Look at all the good things I have given you; take good care

of them, please." Thus, to be a steward is always to be responsive to the trust placed in us by God. The environment, other creatures, and other human beings are not ours; they belong to God. Nevertheless, we have been asked to take care of them and are endowed with the capacities for that care. We are enriched both by those capacities and by those things that are entrusted to us. And so Christians, among other human beings, are asked to care for nature, for the young, the old, the less fortunate, and those unable to care for themselves.

Those who are closely in touch with the stewardship ideal practice stewardship outside the church quite naturally and usually without self-consciousness. These people understand that somehow they are called to care for the employees who work for them. They reach out to peers in the workplace and in social situations not because they have to. If they were asked, they would explain, "It's just the right thing to do." These are also the people who will work hard in a productive enterprise even when no one is looking, not because of an inner-directed guilt but because of an authentic need to respond to trust with trustworthiness. It is people who act out of a sense of response to God's grace, of meeting trust with trustworthiness, who have the fullest understanding of why we also support the church.

Christians support their churches as part of the stewardship of all of life because the church is a vehicle of God's action through Christ in the world. As a vehicle, the church increases the knowledge and love of the Lord. It binds up the wounds of humanity. It teaches men, women, and children what is good by preserving and exchanging the stories of the faith and by providing a context for relationships that make the faith existentially real. The church also offers a place for fellowship, for getting one's brothers and sisters and oneself through life and its struggles by remaining fixed on God and not allowing ourselves to be distracted by goals less worthy than God and life in Christ.

The church merits our support insofar as we can better realize our vocations through the church as children of God. Christians also believe that the church is the one best way to be a disciple or a follower of Jesus. The Navajo people have a nice turn of phrase for describing what happens when one of their number becomes a Christian. They say, "He has gone down the Jesus Road." Early Christians used a similar expression. Amid Roman persecution and tensions with Hellenistic Jews, they spoke in code and called their discipleship after Jesus "the way." In both of

these expressions a sense of direction and perseverance is articulated. Becoming a Christian is not so much a dramatic ontological change like having blue eyes before and brown eyes now as it is an awareness of being different that is characterized mostly by one's different way of being. It is easier to discern who is really a Christian over time than on the basis of surface differences. True Christian disciples evidence their faithfulness in their lives as they try to relate to God by following the acts, teachings, and person of Jesus of Nazareth. So Christian stewardship likewise takes care of that which has been entrusted to us, not by single moments of great passion and generosity but by a long persistence in faithfulness.

## Serious Money

Our understanding of stewardship and financing the needs of congregations starts with the theology of stewardship described here. Yet our understanding is just the beginning. Our compelling interest is that the church be supported adequately to do the right things for the right reasons. Given that interest, a proper understanding of stewardship must be matched with practices of giving and caring that support true discipleship. Understanding and mixing the right ingredients do not, by themselves, make a loaf of bread. Translating the why of stewardship to the how of financing is like the kneading and baking of bread.

We ought to think of providing resources for our Christian congregations as raising serious money. By "serious," I mean two things. First, our gifts of time and money ought to emerge not from being manipulated either by guilt or by fun and games, but rather from a serious consideration of what we as individual Christians and as groups want to do with our time and our resources. The money we raise ought to be serious in another sense as well. If going down the Jesus Road is important to us, truly serious business, then the amounts we gather to do the work of the church in the world ought to be substantial. If people believe that what they are doing in and through their local congregations is deeply important to their lives, then the size of their gifts ought to be larger than their giving to other membership organizations. Moreover, the way that they think about their gifts of time and money ought not to imply the question, "What's the minimum amount I can get away with?"

Seeking after this kind of serious money necessitates that our congregations be worthy of serious support. That is, everything that the
church spends money or effort on ought to be a worthy answer to that
question of the preceding chapter, "What does the Lord require of us?"
We ought not expect that an individual will exercise every aspect of his
or her discipleship after Jesus Christ within a congregational setting. At
times, direct gifts to education, social service agencies, lobbying groups,
seminaries, or mission, relief, and development organizations are wholly
appropriate ways for people to express their love of the Lord and their
obedience to God.

However, if the local church is itself consciously engaged in the
serious business of discipleship, it need have no fear that resources given
to these other good causes will undermine support of the congregation
itself. Indeed, I believe that one of the most common failings of pastoral
leadership today is ministers' tendency to act as though giving to their
churches is the only stewardship game in town. On more than one occasion I have heard pastors decry other kinds of human caring in their
community solely because they weren't sponsored by the church or ap-
peared to compete with church activities. It seemed to me that these
outbursts constituted a striking lack of faithfulness and an extraordinarily
parochial insistence that the work of the church could be realized solely
through the vehicle of church work.

Raising serious money in both the senses I've outlined begins with
theology. We love the Lord, and because God first loved us, we love
one another and make the church a primary vehicle of that love. On a
long and sustained basis people give their time and money to what they
love. A church that lacks adequate funding has one of two problems. It
may be that the community of believers has inadequate resources to
carry out the mission it has constructed for itself. More likely, the believers have a love problem. A love problem exists when the church and
its mission have not captured the hearts of members to a degree sufficient to persuade them to share their resources out of love and a good
feeling about doing so.

It is somewhat easier to understand my argument if we consider the
difference between the ways most people approach sharing resources
with their children and the ways they share resources with their church.
When I buy lunch for my daughter, I may experience companionship,
but I certainly don't make elaborate calculations about why I'm giving

her lunch. I don't do it so that someday she will buy me lunch. I don't do it expecting that if I buy her enough lunches she will take care of me in my old age. No. In the main I spend money on my daughter's lunch because I love her for her own sake and, secondarily, as an extension of myself. Because she is someone whom I love, spending money on her lunch is as pleasant to me as spending money on my own lunch (and probably more so).

By contrast, how often do we hear fellow church members wonder about how much they are giving in relation to the gifts of others? How often does sacrificial giving sound like getting burned? The trick in creating a disposition of giving among a group of people that will produce serious money is to create a climate in which giving to our churches and through our churches to other needs in far-flung places is as natural as buying lunch for a loved one.

Our objective is making a charitable gift that makes us feel good and faithful. No one is ever a cheerful taxpayer, or at least cheerful in the sense of feeling happy about being compelled to fork over a large proportion of income for purposes one has accepted only remotely and indirectly. With taxes there is always a sense that "we" give money to "them." True stewardship can emerge only out of a sense of the self joyfully giving to a larger "us." When all with whom I share are regarded as an extension of me, then no gift I make can be construed as a personal loss. Some people would resist this way of thinking. They might argue that giving until it hurts is what stewardship is all about. But let me ask an old saint's question: How can I love what God loves and not feel joy in caring for it?

## Meeting Givers Where They Can Give

It is a serious mistake for a congregation to allow its need for income to overdetermine the stewardship of its members. People need to give as they are able across the life cycle. Individuals can spot those situations when all the congregation cares about is their money. We all want to be loved for our total selves and not merely for our ability to give. Churches therefore, out of their commitment to personhood, need to learn to be gracious receivers of what people have to offer. If people have time to give, accept it. If a tax accountant is strapped for cash but can donate

his services, accept them, and deploy him on behalf of those who need the services. If a family needs to donate dozens of frozen turkeys, don't say, "We'd really prefer cash." Everybody knows that the church would rather have cash, but maybe turkeys are what these folks have. Ironically, when people experience themselves as being fully valued, they are apt to be freer with their money.

What we have available to give through the church beyond money is highly dependent on the life cycle. People at every stage of life have an innate need to give their gifts in a way that will be recognized by others as a contribution to the community. When the community fails to recognize the gift that is offered, it will also turn away the possibility of future gifts.

Younger adults, those in their 20s, often have more time than money and are seeking meaning and community in their lives. The high-school and college years, which often provide friendship and communal networks, come to an abrupt end when the world of work is joined. Unlike the years of education, when one's work and life meet in a never-ending continuum, private life and work in the adult world tend to be carefully segmented. What to do with oneself after work is a new and sometimes anxiety-provoking question.

Young parents and people with blossoming careers, those in their 30s and 40s, by contrast often have somewhat more money and less time than young adults. But if anything, these people have the emotional need to begin putting something back into the church and social institutions, even while the generations behind and ahead of them seem constantly to be calling on them. Leading Sunday school and using professionally derived skills for good seem to be ways the group in the middle can be productively challenged to give. Having achieved adult competency, these people are just waiting to be asked to use that competency on the church's behalf.

Older people may have more time during weekdays to give of themselves. Many who have lost partners may find Sunday afternoon to be the loneliest time of the week. The church needs to be careful not to arrange all of its activities and opportunities for service at times geared primarily to the needs of its midlife membership. Older adults have time, compassion, skills, and friendship to offer the fellowship in addition to money. The more imaginative use of these skills and energies could enlarge the work of the church, rather than merely get "church work" done (stuffing envelopes and answering phones).

Teens have youthful idealism and boundless energy to offer. The church needs to be careful not to crush it, for while idealism can be unrealistic, it is the source of nearly every good impulse for translating into a life of generosity the values we have taught in the church. Our own experiences of how difficult it is to make the world (or even the local church) a better place must not get translated into the cynical message, "Don't even bother trying."

A stewardship of money will often flow from a stewardship of time, provided two conditions are met. First, the gift of time must be meaningful, connecting the individual or family members to the religious work that they need to do at the time (e.g., grieving a loss or celebrating a birth). Second, the church has to ask for the money. Pastors hate to beg. Almost everyone does. People avoid getting near the stewardship-committee assignment as if it were a bad cold. But a remarkable amount of money is left on the table, or goes to other causes, because the church fails to make its request clearly known to particular people.

You have probably heard the saying that in the typical congregation 20 percent of the members give 80 percent of the money. Recent large-scale studies have borne out this pattern. What they have also shown is that 20 percent of members give virtually nothing. The easy explanations all fail to account for these facts. The top 20 percent of givers are not necessarily the most wealthy. The bottom 20 percent are not predictably the least involved or the poorest. What accounts for these differing levels of generosity?

As previously indicated, some churches just never make the case for giving with some members. These churches fail to ask in a compelling way. At the same time, some potential givers yield to the strong temptation to be free riders, people who receive all services of the fellowship without paying for any. The temptation is understandable, for it is the temptation to be a child—to be taken care of—in one last place in our lives. Adulthood has so many forced commitments of resources. We have to pay for gasoline, for electricity, for food, and for doctors, but no one has to pay for church. Not assuming the responsibility to help pay for church is one way to feel cared for in an uncaring world, to be cared for while being sandwiched between other obligations.

For the most part, free riders and near-free riders have failed to hear the message of a theology of grace discussed earlier in this chapter. They want to be in a place of free grace, to be loved without expectation of

return. Not paying for the services of the church makes an immature person feel as though what has been obtained without cost is that much more sweet. But the truth is that human places of grace depend upon the goodwill of those who dwell in them. At some point the joy of making a contribution to these places needs to be retaught to the adults who are holding back.

More important in many ways than re-educating adults is teaching children the joy of giving early in life. In too many of our congregations, we regard children's giving and volunteering as a nuisance. Carrying out a stewardship program for children produces less income and work than it consumes in resources and energy, to be sure, but its payback period is a lifetime. If we fail to make an early case for stewardship in all its forms, children miss one of the basic lessons in living by grace in God's world. If, on the other hand, we make a visible witness to children in the congregation, we may indirectly find ourselves converting our adult free riders to a more generous pattern of living, although we're talking to the children.

When the church and its leaders get over the hurdle of asking for money, it is helpful to make paying easy for the giver. Monthly bank drafts, credit and debit cards, gifts of appreciated stock, insurance policies with cash values, unused real or personal property—all are ways that people pay for things today. The church needs to accommodate the financial modes that its people use, not force them into the way the church treasurer would like to receive payments. The offering envelope is one of the most outdated symbols of our financing patterns in the church. It belongs to the era of the weekly pay envelope, not to the era of direct deposit and point-of-sale, credit-card-operated gas pumps. Some church treasurers will object that some of these methods take time to set up or (in the case of credit cards) result in reduced receipts. But ask retail business people in your congregation whether they could achieve their sales potential on a cash-only basis. For that matter, congregations might also consider the hidden costs of having to float so much of their programmatic expenses on pledges paid in irregular patterns. Expanding the ways by which people can meet their commitments provides a means to meet those obligations more regularly.

Collecting pledges from current individual income is just one form of accepting the financial stewardship of a congregation's members. But Americans often possess substantial amounts of insurance to honor their

commitments to children and spouses, should they die prematurely. These purchases, designed to soften the impact of a death upon dependents, often create a shield that no one in a family will need later. When a resource is no longer needed for the purpose for which it was originally intended, a great opportunity for stewardship is available. Finding ways to accept what people have to give, *when* they have it to give, is another way to enlarge the generosity of the congregation.

In subsequent chapters we will explore endowments, capital funds, and the roles that fees, rents, bequests, and deferred gifts can play in helping a congregation meet its missional calling more completely with the resources at its collective disposal. But before we leave entirely the subject of giving, let me suggest four questions for our self-examination that can focus all we have discussed in this chapter. To live out a stewardship theology of grace in community, church members need to ask themselves

1. What are you worth to God?
2. What is this congregation's mission worth to you?
3. What do we as a congregation want to be? What will that require of us?
4. What do we have available to give, and when?

Answer those questions with integrity, and financing the congregation ought to seem much more possible.

## Exercises

### What Would Motivate You?

Forget everything you ever heard in a stewardship talk. Why do you give? What would motivate you to give to the work of your church? Your assignment is to come up with a 250-word pitch for supporting your church financially. Your piece, if read on Sunday morning from the front of the church, ought to catch listeners' attention, speak to worthy motivations for giving, and avoid the "fun and games" approach to conning people out of their money.

If you are able to complete the exercise and share your stewardship appeal with others completing the exercise, discuss the patterns that may emerge as you compare individual responses. Are some themes repeated? Do some appeals work only for some people? Does God, the church, grace or gratitude figure prominently in what people would say? How are these stewardship appeals different from those you have heard through the years? How are they the same?

## Telling a Child Why

An alternative version of the first exercise is to come up with a script of similar length for telling a child or children why people ought to give of themselves and their money to the church. Children are concrete thinkers, so it is inadvisable to hide behind code words and jargon. On the other hand, nothing short of a real theological answer (an answer that makes God-sense) will connect God and the offering plate in a child's mind. What would you say? Working with a group and sharing answers, use the same questions as in the prior exercise to analyze responses. What has your group learned about how your congregation ought to ask for support? What has your group learned about how to equip parents for stewardship education?

# CHAPTER 5

# Creating a Commonwealth: Leading the Saints

A congregation, like a country, has its own space, customs, leaders, and culture. Of course, not everything is unique. Just as nations may share values, dominant religions, and legal systems with other lands, particular congregations may share many qualities with other local church cultures. Of course, one way that we can identify a Christian congregation is that it does share a text—the Bible—and an understanding of "how things are" with other such cultures. This is particularly true within denominational family groupings. But being a Southern Baptist or a United Methodist congregation is not like being a McDonald's or a Burger King restaurant; local churches are not just outlets for national brands. No, moving from congregation to congregation is more like moving from the United States to Canada, to New Zealand, and then to Hong Kong. English is spoken in each place, but meanings and customs shift with each move, sometimes radically so.

I like to use the concept of *commonwealth* to denote the distinctive character of every congregation. Each congregation is its own entity with its own resources, leaders, history, myths, visions, and customs. The word commonwealth signals another important dimension of congregational life as well, and that is citizenship. For all of the commonalities with other places, the citizens of a land are responsible for the distinctive shape of the commonwealth. So it is also for churches. There is nothing in mere affiliation that will make a congregation great. Members and leaders of a congregation have to work at their common life, and no one from the outside can do much more than provide guidance. Generosity also characterizes a commonwealth. A commonwealth is, therefore, more than a country, for after all, a country may be a dictatorship, but a commonwealth is by definition a place where the goods of society are shared.

The key questions for a people in a congregation are, then, much like those for citizens of a particular land: What are the practices, understandings, and customs that we will follow to make our land a unique but faithful expression of what it means to be Christian? If each congregation is its own little commonwealth, what makes for a good one? Just as a good country has excellent leaders and enlightened policies, so congregations rise or fall on the quality of their self-understanding, as expressed in leadership, in policies and practices regarding the use of property, in the holding of wealth, and in the employment of people. In the next four chapters, we will discuss these dimensions of congregational life in detail. For now we will turn our attention to one of the central qualities of life as a commonwealth, its character of leadership.

## Leading the Commonwealth

One challenge the contemporary church faces is a crisis in leadership. This crisis is most often depicted as a problem residing in the clergy: ministers just aren't up to the task, goes the popular complaint. As true as that verdict may be, at least most clergy are professionally trained and usually have given considerable time and thought to the nature of their leadership. A far greater scandal for the church is the state of most congregations' lay leadership. Why? Because the typical board of lay leaders operates from one of the most stultifying premises imaginable: that it is like the corporate board that reviews the work of managers to assure board members that a profit is made.

Many of our church boards seem absolutely tone-deaf to the ways in which they might differ from a corporate board, or even from a non-profit organization's board. Two differences are painfully obvious. First, most congregations have little professional staff to oversee. Second, congregations do more than operate through their professional staffs. The work, witness, and care of a congregation are not to be found only in its minister's lists of activities, but in the total *liturgia* or "people-work" of the congregation as the people of God. What the congregation needs in its lay leaders is, therefore, just that—leaders, not supervisors.

Stewards, elders, priests, teachers, evangelists, prophets, and leaders—these are the names given in the Scriptures to the people who lead the people of God. Some of these words sound very much like what we

expect ordained ministers to be today. We want clergy to preach and teach; to administer the rites, sacraments, and ordinances of the church; and to speak out on behalf of God's will in the contemporary social situation. Yet it is good to remember that the people of God have not always possessed a priestly class of leaders and that the Christian church has been most vital at times when its religious leadership has not been wholly concentrated in a single caste of clerics. Most American congregations, of course, are not led solely by pastors or priests.

The great American experiment in popular sovereignty extends to American congregations. Virtually every church has a board of deacons, elders, a consistory, a council, a pastor-parish relations committee, or sometimes simply a board. Yet American ideas about democracy carry additional values beyond the base concern that the people should have a say in their affairs. Regrettably, one of the outcomes of our concepts of leadership in the American context is that we think in terms of checks and balances. The pastor acts; the lay leaders react, as though they were the executive and judicial branches of government.

Running a congregation on the analogy of representative democracy imposes severe limitations on its ministry. Perhaps the greatest of these is that representative processes consign a large portion of the role of lay leaders to the noncreative task of simply saying yes or no. Think for a moment about how often church board meetings revolve around questions that have binary solutions:

"Yes, we can afford it."
"No, it is a nice idea, but it is not in the budget."
"Yes, we can take up a special offering for African relief on the third Sunday in May."

To be sure, these aren't the only kinds of questions that church boards face. Yet I am stunned by the way that they seem to overtake the more creative, life-giving initiatives that lay and clergy religious leadership could be taking on in most places. When leadership is exercised through either assent or veto, it proves to be a very limited form of power indeed.

What is the alternative for American religious congregations? In a word, it is leadership, and not just any leadership but *religious* leadership. Most church boards could benefit from deconstruction of their

secular identities. The accretions of meaning that stick to words like board, council, moderator, president, secretary, and clerk need to be stripped away. In their place, lay leaders need, with their clergy partners, to be challenged by the biblical models for leadership. If the leaders of the people of God are called to be stewards, elders, teachers, evangelists, and prophets, then it is time for self-examination and time for leaders to ask questions like these:

- How are we exercising a ministry of stewardship over the resources we have been given?
- If we are a council of elders who exercise the wisdom of our community, what is this wisdom and are we sharing it?
- If we are called to be teachers, what are we teaching and how are we caring for the souls of those placed in our care?
- If we are to be evangelists, can people tell through our leadership that we believe in the Good News and wish others to possess that Gospel?
- If we are called to be prophets, can we articulate and live the ways in which our faith makes us different and makes a difference in the world around us?

When a board is stuck in "business as usual," questions like these can help it focus upon its more distinctive religious character and orientation. At root, how well we carry out our religious leadership often turns out to be a derivative of our understanding of what we are doing.

The story is told of a man who visits the stoneyard in a cathedral keep. He encounters a man polishing the wing of a beautifully carved limestone angel. He asks the man what he is doing, and the man replies, "I am an artisan, and I'm smoothing the finish work on this piece of limestone." The visitor encounters another man, chipping away at a piece of stone with a chisel. He asks what he's doing, and the man replies, "I'm a rough stonemason, and I'm making the preliminary cuts to put this piece of granite in square." Finally, he encounters an old woman bent over an equally old broom, sweeping up pieces of stone and dirt, and he asks what she is doing. She lifts up her eyes to the visitor, points to the building behind her, and says, "I am building a great cathedral."

If you ask most lay leaders what they are doing on their church boards, I daresay you will get an answer that sounds more like "I'm

cutting stone" than "I'm building a great cathedral." But ponder this: Would it be easier to find people to stand for those offices in our congregations if they believed that what they were doing was something of great moral, creative, and religious worth? Our perspective on lay leadership is the place to start in making that so.

## Seven Ways to Make a Difference

Once we have decided to reorient our perspective on lay leadership in our congregations, certain practices can help us live out our new perspective. Here are seven.

1. *Reclaim the common text as the source of your wisdom.* Christian congregations have a common text, the Bible, from which to draw strength, knowledge, and wisdom. When a board seems to be stumbling around with a secular question like "What is our bottom line here?" turn to the Bible and spend some time asking, "What does this text say about who we are, and who do we want to be?"

2. *Lead the people of God in worship, prayer, and service.* Too often, from the perspective of biblical faith, today's lay leaders concede all sacerdotal activity to the clergy. Even in traditions that reserve special acts and practices within the communities' central worship to ordained clergy, plenty of opportunities arise for lay leaders to lead prayer and witness to their faith in authentic and compelling ways. Perhaps we need to begin thinking of clergy more as symphony conductors than as solo performers. The symphony conductor picks the music but cannot perform it alone. From the bass viol to the finger cymbals, every instrument needs a player to make the symphony come alive. In a similar way, our congregations are potentially full of much greater religious vitality if we will learn to use all the instruments that wait to be sounded.

3. *Lead toward religious goals, not toward physical goals.* As important as it is to balance a budget or to complete an educational wing, each is but a means toward more important religious ends. We balance a budget because it helps to continue the work of Christian witness and nurture in a faithful and enduring way. We build an expanded

educational wing not because we like beautiful buildings, but because it is a physical foundation for the nurture of souls. If we remind ourselves of the moral ends that the means we discuss will help us achieve, then we may find ourselves making decisions on church boards about the use of means different from what might otherwise be the case.

4. *Exercise stewardship to increase talents, not merely to preserve them.* Ending the year in the black, saving something for a rainy day, and even putting a new roof on the parsonage seem to be trivial goals when we are faced with the ways Jesus talked about people who go after lost sheep or lost coins and give up all that they have for the sake of God's reign. Yet when the stewardship of things, including property and money, is linked to higher aims, we become paradoxically freer and more productive in their use. Few people would want to give money to replace something just because it was old. But putting a new coat of paint on the walls of the sanctuary so that it might be a beautiful place to worship is a superior motivation that attracts giving. And what is true for buildings is true sevenfold for missions. No one will give to maintain the same budget as last year, but many will give that someone might eat, read, or live and grow in the name of Jesus Christ.

5. *Evangelize.* Would you tell the people in your work or other social setting that you are a leader in your church? Why or why not? To be a leader ought to mean demonstrating the truth of the Gospel for your whole life in a way that it is transparently obvious to others, even if they do not themselves believe. Anything that takes as much time and effort as serving on a church board ought to make a difference for the better in the board member's life. What one says, and how one says it, although differing from person to person, nevertheless makes the strongest witness the lay leader can offer both within and outside the faith community.

6. *Take responsibility for the souls of others.* Again, this task may seem to be the pastor's work. Yet to be in a position of any authority within the community of faith is to take on the burden of caring for others. When lay leaders find a fellow congregation member in turmoil over a relationship, a work situation, or a sense of doubt about his or her place in the universe, they need to rise to the trust placed in them by their selection and demonstrate the love of God as best they can with the

tools and trust they have been given. In American middle-class culture, praying with and for people in trouble often seems awkward and difficult, yet as any competent pastor will acknowledge, it is both one of the most intimate and most desired things that a human being hopes for and needs from his or her brother and sisters.

7. *Model discipleship.* In some congregations, lay leadership is divided into lesser and greater boards. Perhaps the deacons do the caring and self-giving work of tending to the sick and poor, while elders, vestry members, or trustees attend to finances. Truly, however, if we are called to be disciples of Jesus Christ, then all who would be great among us, who would be leaders, must become the servants of all. A servant leader, or a leader who acts as a disciple, will not eschew acts of caring and prefer the privilege of controlling the purse strings. Indeed, churches whose lay leadership is actively involved in caring for the homebound and homeless, one-on-one in the name of Jesus Christ, are destined to make more Christlike decisions when they gather to meet about financial concerns.

# Exercise

### Leadership Retreat

Your pastor is after you to help out. He says, "I'd like for you to come up with three passages in the Bible that help model what our congregation's leadership ought to be about and lead a discussion on the passages at next month's retreat." After trying to duck the assignment and put the work back on the pastor (after all, *he* went to seminary), you agree and develop an interest in biblically inspired models of church leadership. Which three passages do you choose and why? In what ways do these portions of Scripture offer a word of judgment on your congregation's present patterns of leadership? In what ways do they offer a word of empowerment?

# CHAPTER 6

# Practices of the Commonwealth Congregation: The Church as Landlord

It really should not be surprising that people who do not know how to talk about money with one another should have a hard time managing their common affairs. Still, one wonders about some of the practices that are common in contemporary churches. Chief among these confused practices are those related to the use of church property, the management and expenditure of other assets, the salary and benefits of clergy and other church workers, and (as we have seen) the leadership of the people of God. Thinking in terms of a commonwealth helps with all of these matters, for when business practices are not thought to be intrinsic to the life and identity of congregations, they are often undertaken in a fashion contrary to the common interests of that body. Once again, it is useful to see congregations as little commonwealths. A commonwealth has foreign and internal relations. People want to know about a place. Is it a good neighbor? Is it a good place to live and work? The same questions apply to congregations. In this chapter, we consider one way in which the congregation enacts its common life—through the management and use of its property.

## Charging Appropriately for Services and Building Use

"How much should we charge?" is a question many congregations find themselves asking when a potential tenant proposes to use the congregation's building. Unfortunately, it's just one question among many that should have come earlier in a congregation's evaluation of providing shelter or hospitality to outside groups. Consider the following scenario:

Highland Valley Church has a problem making ends meet—a surprising state of affairs for a church whose parking lot seems always to be

full. On Sundays, there's worship and Sunday school in the morning, while two youth groups meet in the evening. Monday through Friday, the Christian education wing is packed with First Beginnings, a day-care center. Founded as a church-related nursery school 30 years ago by a former pastor's wife, it has become a full-day early-childhood program catering mostly to the working poor and single mothers. Up on the third floor is Bible Press, an offshoot of yet another former pastor's ministry, which markets by direct mail both Bible study aids and trips to the Holy Land. Monday through Friday nights the fellowship hall and adult Sunday school rooms are occupied by a variety of Scout and 12-step groups, numbering eight in all. Wednesday is choir night. Members coming for choir practice might also encounter the clients of the pastoral counselor, who uses the former associate pastor's study.

Highland Valley Church's leadership doesn't know what to make of this beehive of activity. Some council leaders point to the level of their church's building use with great pride, saying, "Just look at the hospitality our church offers to this community." Others aren't so sure that the blessing of busyness is all it's cracked up to be. They point out that the floor is often sticky, and that the building retains the aroma of little children and day-old smoke. The women's association has, on more than one occasion, complained that the kitchen is always a mess.

Highland Valley's new pastor also knows just how busy the church building is. He recently set out to offer a midweek Bible study, only to learn that all the rooms were spoken for. This discovery has caused him to question whether the church is making appropriate use of its facilities or whether outside groups have overbalanced the congregation's own interests. Church member Etta Cromwell points out that the Scouts, Alcoholics Anonymous, and First Beginnings are all good forms of outreach.

Now, on top of everything else, an unexpected increase in the church's insurance bill has created a budgetary crunch. The cause of the increased bill turns out to be the insurance company's decision to rate churches with weekday child-care programs separately from those without. Meanwhile, the church faces the need for a new roof, increased costs for utilities and medical coverage for employees, and the desire to keep its youth-ministry intern on staff after she graduates from seminary. Everything, it seems, that congregations do costs money.

All of the groups that use the church have one thing in common. They pay no rent. Given the church's financial problems, some congregational leaders believe that outside groups should pay rent. However,

they diverge in their views as to whether the church should charge only the extra amount of janitorial services and utilities that a group requires or a share of the larger cost of keeping the church open. Other church leaders worry that presenting a bill for services will strain their relationships with community groups. At this point, debate about the outside-group issue has become so acrimonious that the council is looking for a way out by finding savings elsewhere in the budget. Right now council members are considering, as an economy measure, cutting the church secretary's hours in half.

Problems like the ones faced by Highland Valley Church often arise from the failure to think appropriately about the congregation as an entity with material assets. Just as individual human beings have bodies, material possessions, and needs, so too most congregations have physical expressions that embody their spiritual and communal identity. Here are some of the most common ways congregations disorder the relationship between their assets and purposes:

1. Perhaps the greatest problems related to church building use by outside groups stem from the failure of leaders to consider the relation of the outside group's activity to the mission of the church.
2. Many congregations fail to think about the cost of having an asset at all. At least once a church's mortgage is burned (or other debt is retired), it seems as though the building, camp, or bus is there to be used, free of charge.
3. Congregations also get in trouble by letting the first tenant set the de facto rates for all others. Often then, because the first group paid little or nothing, subsequent groups pay little or nothing for the use of the church, an outcome stemming from a misconstrued sense of fairness.
4. Congregations sometimes confuse loyalty to members with the interests of the church. Thus a quilting group, a rock band, or the catering business of a valuable church member can become the no-rent tenant that produces no tangible benefit for the church itself.
5. Congregations also find themselves in trouble because they think about cost in inappropriate ways. Economists distinguish between average cost, marginal cost, and opportunity cost. With average cost, the total cost of doing business is distributed proportionally among the activities within the enterprise. With marginal cost, the

concern is how much it costs the organization to add another activity to the mix. With opportunity cost, the question centers on the cost of a lost benefit if a congregation commits to doing one thing rather than some alternative activity. In dealing with outside groups, congregations need to weigh all of these costs and select the appropriate ones to evaluate the costs and benefits of hosting a particular activity or group.

Thinking in terms of commonwealth enables the congregation and its leaders to think about the church building as a shared asset. Both parts of that term are helpful to reflect upon. As an asset, a form of wealth, its use ceases to be a trivial matter, something to be taken for granted in the way we once regarded clean air and water when we believed their supply to be limitless. Viewing the building as a shared asset, one sees that what is held in common must be used to benefit the common interests of the congregation's members. From there, it is but a small step to the really important questions. First, "What are the best uses to which we can put this building (or camp, or bus), which we hold in common?" When we begin posing our questions in terms of what is "best," we need to define best in terms of the church's total mission. Here is where "counting the cost" of our decisions in terms of opportunity costs can help make a difference in pursuing our mission. When congregations allow themselves to be boxed in by obligations to existing tenants, they may miss opportunities to use their buildings for more important purposes.

On the other hand, congregations need to be careful not to evict groups from their buildings thoughtlessly. For this reason, congregations may decide to draw up formal contracts for building use, however simple, with definite expiration dates, and to develop a process by which a group's use of the congregation's shared assets is evaluated by the congregation for "missional fit" far in advance of renewing the contract. This process would give congregations an opportunity to ask questions about the best use of their facilities, while allowing tenant groups a longer lead time in finding suitable quarters, should their leases not be extended.

Congregations need also to look at ways in which building users might shoulder some of the costs of tenancy. Most groups have some money and can pass along to their members small charges for building

use. Subsidies ought to be provided when a group's mission is a true extension of the church's mission, but the full average cost of hosting the group ought to be stated. Sometimes groups with very little income of their own are related to larger support institutions, such as the United Way or federal, state, or local governments, that can, and expect to, help community-serving groups pay the cost of the physical space they use. Appropriately stating the cost of hosting a group can thus be the first step in recovering the legitimate costs of its occupation. At the very least, quantifying the cost of a particular group's use of space and services can help a congregation ask the missional question: Is hospitality for this activity important enough to our mission as Christ's church in this particular place that we want to expend our resources for this purpose?

Too often groups in the not-for-profit world live by passing on their costs to someone else. One must be especially suspicious of for-profit entrepreneurs who, for example, tutor youth or provide respite care for Alzheimer's patients in a church building. At the very least, a church has an obligation to satisfy itself that it feels good about what is taking place on its premises.

Knowing when to use average cost versus marginal cost, let alone opportunity cost, can be difficult. What proportion of the total cost of operation should be allocated to the Boy Scout troop versus the Sunday morning worship service, for instance? In general, groups that can pay, or whose clients can pay, or that are supported by some entity that will pay for them, should never be asked to share less than the marginal cost of their use of space. On the other hand, a church should expect to go out of pocket to a greater or lesser extent for activities that are intrinsic to its mission, such as feeding the hungry or providing meeting space for its own youth group.

A final important dimension to setting costs applies to entrepreneurs. A simple formula for determining the appropriate rent for such tenants begins with the appropriate market rent for the particular kind of space, with adjustments for access, limitations (if any), and attached services (such as being on the church's switchboard or voice mail), less a deduction for the intrinsic benefit that having the activity within the congregation's building brings to the congregation. For example, a congregation might well estimate that a pastoral counselor would have to pay $300 a month for space in a comparable building but also consider that her being located within the commonwealth of this congregation is a

benefit worth $100 a month. Thus it might set a discounted rent of $200 per month for office rental.

## Exercise

### Counting the Costs

How much do you know about where your congregation gets its money and where it spends it? In this exercise we look at building use from the standpoint of the congregation's mission and identity. First, write down in a few short sentences what you think the mission of your congregation is. Second, find out about all the uses to which your congregation's building, grounds, and other assets are put. Do any of the groups that use the church pay rent? Could they or should they? (Some homework may be necessary to complete this second part of the exercise.) Third, using a grid or other device for comparison, compare how your congregation's use of its assets meets or fails to meet its missional priorities. Finally, assuming that you can change mission and asset use, what changes might be in order for your congregation to better match its operations to its priorities? How might you make necessary changes?

# CHAPTER 7

# Practices of the Commonwealth Congregation: Holding Wealth

Every ongoing community holds resources to support its common life. These resources can be as concrete and simple as a village's fishing nets, or as vast and complex as a large university's endowment portfolio. All human institutions have these resources, but being part of the church poses a particular moral challenge to all Christian institutions that gather, have, and hold endowments. That issue is how and when it is legitimate for one part of the body of Christ to build up treasures where moth and rust do corrupt. As soon as a congregation begins holding any form of wealth, it is vital that it have a clear, theologically justifiable answer to the question, "What is the purpose of your endowment?" Thankfully, the history of the Christian churches offers us theological and ethical resources out of which we might craft responses to the "purpose of endowment" challenge. Along the way, the concept of commonwealth proves enormously helpful, for in the end, the holding of wealth by any part of the church is justified only if it benefits the common life and ministry of the body of Christ.

## History

I first began to think more deeply about endowments and wealth-holding when I was asked to meet with a group of endowed parishes to discuss the history, theology, and ethics of church endowments. The first thing that struck me upon reflection was how curious it was, when viewed from the whole of church history, that there should be an affinity group for endowed parishes. In the long course of Christian history most churches were endowed churches. To be sure, we read about voluntary

collections in the New Testament era supporting the apostles and the communal sharing of incomes and personal wealth to enable gatherings of early Christians to support one another.

Fairly early, however, and certainly by the time of Constantine, the organized church was financing its ministry by what were, in effect, endowments. In the Western church for more than a millennium, a priest could not be ordained to the pastoral office without a benefice, or a living, supporting that office. Without an endowment to support the pastorate, no job was available and thus no ordination was possible. If that were still the practice, each ordained minister would be entitled to the income from a piece of land and the service of its serfs, inherited from the previous tenant of that pastoral office. Alternatively, if you had a rich father who wanted you to be a priest, your family could bestow upon the church a gift adequate to your support for the rest of your natural life. In either case, the support of organized Christianity's most costly expense, personnel, was achieved by a capital investment. Relief for the poor might be accomplished by almsgiving, and church-building was typically financed by gifts from regional nobility. Still, normal church finance was endowment-based. The pastoral office, with its requirement of a benefice was assumed. The clergy were a form of landed gentry.

Sometimes during those years, to be sure, this assumption clashed with other emergent ecclesiologies (ways of being the church), beliefs, and church practices. The most challenging of these other ways of being Christian was the calling to assume voluntary poverty. The Spiritual Franciscans took this principle as far as they could. They read their Bibles to mean that the Christ who said, "Do not worry . . . about what you will wear. . . . Consider the lilies of the field," (Matt. 6:25-28) did not himself worry about such things—to the point that he did not own the tunic for which gamblers cast lots at his crucifixion. Christian discipleship for these Spiritual Franciscans meant Christlike behavior at all times. They believed, therefore, that they too needed to reject private property.

Umberto Eco's great novel *The Name of the Rose* has a scene in which the Franciscans' leader is debating with the Vatican's apostolic delegate over just this matter. After days they haven't gotten anywhere on the tunic issue, so the Vatican's representative comes up with this compromise: "Well, at least, gentlemen, I think we can all agree that Christ had a purse." The opposing worldviews within Christendom were

so profoundly different that the propertied institutional church could not even comprehend how church life could be different, or how the Franciscans could be up to anything other than committing heresy and killing the church. The Franciscans, meanwhile, thought that the church's great wealth undermined its discipleship and that the church's possession of property could not but lead to abuse. The Inquisition ended up torturing the Franciscans for their thought crimes against property.

I dwell on the episode because the abuse of the material dimension of church life was a key factor in Martin Luther's initiation of the Reformation. Luther's 95 theses scored a crucial blow for the view that the authority of the church is subordinate to the authority of the Scriptures. It took several centuries for the biblical principles unleashed by the Reformation to exert a serious effect on patterns of church finance. Pastorates and particular churches continued to be supported by land wealth, and the clergy continued to be treated as lesser nobility. Even when the churches of England, Scotland, and Germany were transplanted to America, they brought with them the expectation that land (which was, after all, the chief form of capital prior to the Industrial Revolution) would finance their ministries. Throughout the 18th and 19th centuries Anglicans, Presbyterians, and Roman Catholics in the old South supported their ministers by leasing out glebe lands (plots yielding revenue to a parish church or pastorate) and, until 1865, the slaves to go with those lands. Then, as now, to be attached to a source of capital assured one of resources but not of righteousness.

What happened to change the pattern of church support was a twofold revolution in values beginning just 200 years ago in the then new United States. The first aspect of this revolution in values was the rise of a conception of the ministry that might be termed "evangelical." Previously, only the Protestant sects of Quakers, Anabaptists, and other so-called free churches believed that common people should return to New Testament patterns of gathering churches and supporting ministers out of the resources of a particular community. But by 1800 virtually everyone but the Unitarians in Boston was accepting the idea of calling men (and occasionally women) into Christian service without asking them to be gentlemen first and well-supported second. In less than a generation, the typical minister went from being a gentlemen in a starched white collar at study in the parsonage to being a circuit-riding preacher visiting the back country in torn and mud-spattered clothes.

The second great development of the 19th century affecting how people financed and regarded their churches was the rise of the middle classes. Prior to the ascendance of the bourgeoisie—those small-business people, merchants, and white-collar workers who still fill mainline Protestant churches in America—the class structure of the United States virtually guaranteed that any given community or church was made up of the propertied wealthy and the working poor. The wealthy had most of their resources tied up in land; the poor had little to give. But when the middle classes began to expand, most of their resources were in current income, or wages. Church finance rapidly caught up with its clientele's resources; and monthly subscriptions, offering envelopes, and proportional tithing replaced a former reliance on status-priced pew rents and land proceeds. A wholesale change took place in less than 50 years in the middle of the 19th century.

Another change brought on by this revolution in values was that certain biblical texts were recovered from near-oblivion to create a theology of stewardship. The widow's mite reflected the democratizing effects of the evangelical conception of the church's ministry. Everyone was good enough to support the church, and everyone's sacrificial gift had merit in the eyes of God. At the same time, the historically dubious practice of tithing was recovered from Leviticus and made normative for people living half a world and 28 centuries away. To the new emphasis on proportional tithing was added a New Testament gloss, in which Jesus could be heard to say, "Every one to whom much is given, of him much will be required" (Luke 12:48, RSV).

The striking thing to me, as someone who studies these matters, is how quickly the church adjusted to the changed market realities surrounding its members and supporters. Somewhere in those developments of the 19th century, however, the central theological difficulty was obscured in the rush to income-based tithing. The enduring issue is materiality—what do we do with any of our resources, we who are in the love and care and providence of God?

Pretty soon the adjustment to the market realities of middle-class, wage-earning church members became a self-perpetuating ideology of church support that stressed the virtues of income-based stewardship and still failed to grapple with the full theological problem of our being embodied spirits in God's world. Balancing the Sermon on the Mount's admonition not to worry about material things with Jesus' adjacent recognition that "the Lord knows you need these things" is the real issue

that catches us again and again. We are material beings with lots of things and needs, whether or not we want to think about them.

Mostly, the 19th-century church taught its members to duck the problem by accepting prevailing economic patterns as given. The 19th- and 20th-century mainline church made its peace with an income-based provision of resources for the church's ministry, and from the time of the Social Gospel onward it was suspicious of wealth and its uses. As the reader knows by now, material resources are, for me, all part of the same pie—be it income or wealth, it's God's stuff, not ours. But the mainline church tended to think otherwise, proclaiming wealth bad, income good; capital bad, labor good; profit evil but wages excellent. The church for close to a century has labored under a wretched understanding of economics and a poor theology of human economic activity.

As part of its critique of accumulated capital, a critique of endowments arose. Some of the most common objections are these:

- A church with an endowment is a curse to its members, whose desire to give and whose personal stewardship is undermined.
- The fate of European state churches shows that churches are healthier when they have to rely on voluntary gifts, not endowments.
- The church should live by the faith of its current members, not from the interest of its dead members' monies.
- Endowments simply encourage preachers and staff to disregard the wishes of the membership.
- An endowment always depresses per-member giving.
- To gather endowments is to show faithlessness in God's ability to provide, just as the ancient Israelites showed their faithlessness when they tried to collect more than a day's manna in the wilderness.
- God demands that we be spendthrift in love. Building an endowment is like holding back on our neighbors, as Ananias and Sapphira did in Acts 5.
- Since endowments usually come from wealthy people, they simply make the church a party to tainted money and ill-gotten gains.
- Endowments give priority to yesterday's buildings, programs, and plans over the mission to which God may be calling the church today.

With all of that criticism, it is a wonder that anyone would dare utter the word "endowment" in a contemporary church. Nevertheless, I am hopeful that we can help overturn some of that old "conventional foolishness" with a more complete appreciation of stewardship that extends to the use of all resources placed at our personal and corporate disposal.

## A Means Toward Sharing

One way to start in countering the anti-endowment sentiment is by showing where income-based strategies for financing religious activity are inadequate to the tasks before us. There is a trap in the current income-based approach to support of the ministry: it predicates the provision of ministry on the ability to pay. One thing endowments can do is to shift financial support for ministry from those who do not have means to those who do have the means to support ministry. The shift may be an intergenerational one in which grandparents in effect guarantee that there will be a church for their grandchildren's generation. It might also be a geographical shift whereby Christians in north suburban Chicago set up a fund with their means to provide a steady flow of support to a fledgling Christian college in Zambia. In either case, the endowment is being used to accomplish the purpose of sharing the faith by sharing resources. The endowment becomes a vehicle of ministry, not an end in itself.

Another way in which the old reliance on middle-class wage tithing is unhelpful to the contemporary church is in its failure to recognize that many of us have built up considerable safety nets of resources to carry us through what might befall us in life, but we'll have no need for those resources beyond the grave. Increasingly, the middle class has a stewardship problem with capital. That is, we possess capital in amounts greater than most of our forebears could have imagined, and thus we have something new over which to exercise stewardship. Our colleges, hospitals, and other not-for-profits will be happy to help us deal with that problem, but the churches have been slow to break out of their capital/endowment fear to suggest ways in which we may support the Gospel after we are gone and support Christ's mission after we are fully with Christ.

It is not enough, however, to make a negative case against an over-reliance on current member income for financing mission. We need to

make a positive theological and ethical case for endowments and, having made the case, make sure that our current practices measure up to that ideal. Here is where the concept of commonwealth re-enters the picture. Endowments, at their best, are a form of commonwealth, for what are they but capital in a particularly moral form? By moral form, I refer to the fact that endowments are capital held in trust for the particular common purposes of a group of people, in this case the church. They derive their value not from their size, nor from their growth and return rates, but from the purposes for which the wealth is deployed. The term commonwealth thus reminds us that an endowment held by a congregation is wealth, and yet the beneficiary of the wealth is not a private individual but a community.

People with social consciences, including most clergy, have drunk deeply at the well of suspicion about wealth. It is, therefore, necessary to articulate ways in which church wealth can be moral. One of the easiest analogies I have found to support the idea that an endowment is both a form of commonwealth and an ethical vehicle is the church building. Very few churches in our country exist without buildings where the community gathers to worship and from which members mount their programs of witness, fellowship, and service. Often members make those buildings available to a wide variety of community groups. Alcoholics, people in recovery, homeless people, parents who have lost a child, Boy Scouts, and Girl Scouts all find a warm, well-lighted place to meet and thus share in the commonwealth of a particular congregation.

Buildings are a form of property, an asset, just as surely as stocks and bonds are assets. Even if a building is open only for the worship of the faithful on Sundays, something useful is being done in the name of God. When it comes to church buildings, no one would argue that the roof should be allowed to cave in because holding buildings is wrong. Instead, the asset is maintained for the good it can do both now and in the future. Likewise, endowments ought to be viewed as a form of asset supporting the ministry of the church.

There sometimes comes a time, however, when the building does not fit what goes on inside its walls. We are all familiar with the older, mostly urban congregations that are slaves to slate roofs and utility bills, whose ministry is encumbered by a white-elephant building. Endowments and the investment policies associated with them can also be mismatched with the ministries they support or, like church buildings,

can become ends in themselves. Yet that danger, I would argue, is no reason not to have an endowment. Rather, it is a challenge to the stewards of any asset—physical or financial—to become more conscientious.

Our biblical faith is helpful to us at this point. Jesus' teachings about the use of talents, about not burying those talents, come to mind, of course (Matt. 28:14-30). So too do his warnings about not building bigger barns when our lives are at stake (Luke 12:13-21). Yet the passage that has been much on my mind for our time is the one in which a woman opens costly perfume and rubs it over Jesus' feet with her hair (Mark 14:3-9; John 12:1-8). Judas is quick to say, "Why was the ointment wasted in this way? [It] could have been sold for more than three hundred denarii, and the money given to the poor" (Mark 14:4).

That story is on my mind because it sounds so much like our modern in-church battles about what we do with our assets. Judas is playing the role of grumpy treasurer, or perhaps social-action committee chair, complaining that restoring the stained-glass windows is a huge waste when there are so many homeless people in the streets. Actually, the gospel writer John thinks that it is more likely that Judas was looking to line his own pockets. Yet hear what Jesus says: "You always have the poor with you, but you do not always have me" (John 12:8). He also says, "She has done a good service for me" (Mark 14:6). His words introduce a complexity to the stewardship of things that we hadn't expected. Sometimes you celebrate; most days you take care of the poor. Sometimes you kill the fatted calf; most days you work in the field.

The crucial and difficult thing to know is when to conserve and when to expend without reserve. Christ's many economic analogies and encounters urge us to discern a path between the twin dangers of being misers and being profligates. This is hard news for those of us who wish that our fiduciary responsibilities could be discharged by following rules by rote without exercising spiritual discernment. But the ethics of endowments and of all aspects of stewardship in Christian institutions requires a continuing concern for fitting our resources to what God is calling us to do and be as a people. I think this concern means four concrete things for our stewardship of endowments in the church. These four are the theological and ethical criteria for assessing our faithfulness in holding wealth for the body of Christ.

## A Theology of Grace

The first criterion is that we who have or are seeking to develop endowments possess a theology of grace that can lighten the burden of discerning how to manage faithfully the things placed in our care. Grace is always about a gift you did not earn. It is easy to fall into the sin of pride when your institution has more resources than others. Usually there is little factual basis for pride, since endowments are mostly the result of someone's past affection for an institution translated into a trust placed in its future. As such, the size of an endowment is not a current market valuation like a stock price. (It would be unfitting to say that my seminary is currently worth $170 million, even though its endowments total that amount.) No, the endowments we hold are more like an honor placed upon a boy by a dying father. The boy hopes to be worthy of what he has already been given. Likewise our worth as institutions is judged by the fruits we bear.

As Christians, we are supposed to live by grace. But how often do we demonstrate grace as the foundation of our lives? Endowments should be a reminder of blessing and should give us permission to live faithfully and graciously.

## Communally Understood Purpose

A fair amount has been written about whether churches should use an endowment for building, staff support, or outside mission. The important thing is not which answer a congregation adopts, but rather the theological and moral narrative it tells itself about this commonwealth it holds. The church with an endowment, but without a communally understood purpose for that endowment, is a church headed for trouble. But it isn't good enough simply to have a narrative about the purpose of one's endowment. The story also has to hold up as good theology.

For instance, I am aware of a church in a major city whose commonwealth was dedicated to preserving the great religious art legacy of Europe. The congregation used its endowment regularly to acquire stunning art. Yet when several candidates who interviewed for the church's pastorate asked about economic justice, community involvement, and the use of church members' considerable power to advance missional

concerns, they got blank stares from the pastoral nominating committee. That church had a narrative, but one that contained no Christian charity. Its wealth did not help it be a better church, but it sure made for a great religious art collectors' club.

On the other hand, I know of an Episcopal parish in Indianapolis that has made great strides in outreach and vital mission by allocating its endowment to building upkeep and basic operating expenses. The story there says, "The lights and bulletins are paid for; the rest is up to us. What are we going to do with this gift? Every dollar we give goes directly into the mission of the church." That, I submit, is a much healthier communally shared understanding. The commonwealth there has a clear purpose and advances the congregation's mission.

## Spending Rates

Directly related to the issue of a communally understood purpose is that of setting a spending rate that matches the purpose of the endowment. I have been on the inside of a number of institutions, including local churches, that fought over how much of the endowment to spend each year. It is a matter of ethical integrity that a church establish a spending rate for its endowment. Here again, several options are defensible. A church that has a purpose that is virtually eternal (such as building maintenance) might set a fairly low rate of spending so that the real value of the endowment might keep pace with inflation and still be able to defray basic building expenses 30 years from now. The purpose of the commonwealth in this case would be to free the congregation for worship and mission, and the spending rate would be appropriate.

At the other extreme, a church might, through the bequest of a donor, have a quasi-endowment fund that required it to spend the corpus and income over a 20-year period for education and recreation for youth in the neighborhood. The purpose is to help the next generation of youth in the hope that they will subsequently be able to do their part. A low spending rate in that case of, say, 4.5 percent would be inconsistent with the purpose of the fund. A church holding too much or too little back for the future is living in such a way that its ethics don't match its moral sense of what the money is for. This fact should be obvious, but how often have we heard old maxims like "Never invade principal" or "Use

all the income" quoted to replace genuine reasoning about what the purposes of endowed or quasi-endowed funds are and what spending rates fit those purposes? Of course, it is essential to respect donor restrictions, but ideally, before the gift is even made, donors and recipient organizations should have a clear sense of the commonwealth they are creating. Being constructively up-front about these matters serves as a model of trust in Christian community.

**Investment Policies**

Finally, among ethical criteria that go with having an endowment, consider the matter of investment policies. Once again, there are "fitting" and "unfitting" ways to make money for particular Christian missions. A powerful argument in our investment culture is the extreme position that any social or ethical investment screen is a violation of the fiduciary responsibility to seek maximum return. But upon examination, this totally laissez-faire stance is flawed. If your church treasurer offered to get you a 22 percent return with his uncle Louie, who owned a string of prostitution ranches in Nevada and was looking to expand, you probably wouldn't invest, even though it was a legal investment and the risk exposure was negligible. Why? Because that way of making money implicates us in the evil way it is made. You cannot have the purpose of feeding the hungry or preaching the Gospel and pay for it with the proceeds from the sexual humiliation of young women in Nevada.

Usually, the choices of good and bad investments aren't so clear, but the way we make and expand the wealth portion of our commonwealths says a great deal about who we are. Surely, we should look to avoid vice, but our congregations ought also to challenge their endowment managers to find positive investment choices that are consistent with our beliefs and purposes. If you can invest in a firm that makes a beneficial product, pays a good rate of return, and treats its employees fairly, buy it; for when you do, you will have made a witness about the kinds of players you value in the marketplace. Above all, our investment policies can and ought to advance, not undermine, the witness of the church of Jesus Christ.

Holding some wealth in common in the form of endowments is a time-honored practice for supporting the church. Our theology challenges

us to expand our conception of stewardship to embrace all that we are and hold in the name of God with a sense of grace. And ethically, we practice our faith when we create commonwealth holdings consistent with the tasks of ministry before us.

# Exercise

### Endowment by Fiat

"Goodness, we've just been left a million dollars," the minister of your church declares one Saturday morning while you share a cup of coffee in the church office and he absentmindedly opens the mail. The attorney's notice of a bequest with no strings attached leads to the next surprise of the day. The pastor turns to you and says, "I want you to lead a group to tell us what we should do with this gift." You have been given, almost by fiat, the opportunity to think with other leaders about the future of your church and its resources, and the opportunity to create (or expand) an endowment. What purpose should this fund have? How should the bequest be invested? How should it be spent? How do you communicate these policies and preferences to the congregation in a way that enhances and does not diminish its common life? Does knowing what you would do with a bequest make you (or anyone else) any more interested in making a similar bequest?

# CHAPTER 8

# The Servants Are Worth Their Wages:
# Congregations as Employers

I am constantly amazed at how low clergy salaries are, as a group, in contemporary American churches. Clearly clergy are not paid on the basis of the hours they work or the difficulty of the jobs they do. Nor are they paid on the basis of the preparation required for the job. What more difficult profession can one imagine than one in which a minister must be an administrator of personnel and finance matters, a gifted public speaker, a coordinator of volunteers, a pastoral presence when people are in crisis, and a spiritual leader of a community?

The typical American congregation—that is, any but the smallest—is as complex an institution as a small business, with the decision-making apparatus of a medium-size not-for-profit corporation. It also has an important overlay that makes its work different: the work being done is God's work, and thus a matter of life and death, of spirit and compassion. Recruits to the armed forces some years ago were offered "the toughest job you will ever love." Most clergy would identify with that slogan. The Bureau of Labor Statistics (BLS) each year produces an *Occupational Outlook Handbook*. Each handbook entry describes a job or vocational pursuit in the stark and neutral terms that a high school guidance counselor might use to help a student evaluate one profession over another. The entry on working conditions for the clergy is instructive:

> Members of the clergy typically work long and irregular hours. Of those who served full time as clergy, about one-third spent at least 60 hours a week on their duties. Although many of their activities are sedentary and intellectual in nature, they are frequently called upon at short notice to visit the sick, comfort the dying and their families, and provide counseling to those in need. Involvement in

community, administrative, and educational activities may require clergy to work evenings, early mornings, holidays, and weekends. (Bureau of Labor Statistics, *Occupational Outlook Handbook, Dictionary of Occupational Titles,* 120.107-010)

The BLS description of what clergy do ends with a warning that "individuals considering a career in the clergy should realize they're choosing not only a career but a way of life," adding that clergy should be "capable of making difficult decisions, working under pressure, and living up to the moral standards set by their community." For all this difficult work, the average Protestant minister could expect to take home $20,000 (in 1993 dollars), and the average Roman Catholic priest could expect to receive about $9,000 in direct cash compensation. When such benefits as insurance and housing were added, the figures for Protestant and Catholic clergy rose to $40,000 and $29,000, respectively.

The amounts paid to, and for the benefit of, Protestant and Catholic clergy are not themselves alarming. But when the clergy as a group are compared to other groups such as lawyers, teachers, and educational administrators—people who have professional training and responsibilities for the care or formation of others—clergy fare rather poorly. During the 1995-96 school year the average salary of all public elementary- and secondary-school teachers in the United States was $37,900. Meanwhile, elementary-school principals who oversaw a "flock" of about the same number of individuals as a typical Protestant congregation were making average salaries during the 1996-97 school year of $62,900. No profession is currently more glutted than that of the law, but despite keen competition for jobs, the median salaries of lawyers six months after graduation in 1996 was $40,000. For public- interest lawyers, that portion of the profession ostensibly most motivated by altruism, the figure for recent graduates was $30,000. The median annual salary of all lawyers for the same year hovered around $60,000. The ministry in the 1990s, as a profession, paid very little when compared to other professions, in particular to those for which postgraduate preparation is normally required (Bureau of Labor Statistics, *Occupational Outlook Handbook*).

It has not always been the case that clergy fared so poorly in the marketplace. In a study of clergy income, I examined ministers' incomes against changes in wage and price levels over more than 120 years. The

ministers were all from the various denominational streams that joined over time to form the present-day United Methodist Church. What I discovered was that, from a high point in 1960 when the ministers' mean income nearly equaled median family income in the United States, real clergy income spiraled downward after 1968 to the point that by the late 1970s clergy made less than half of what a typical middle-class American family earned in a year. Moreover, while clergy incomes more than maintained purchasing power relative to inflation across the century, they did not grow at a rate approaching the economy as a whole. Thus, while the American standard of living soared and a vast proportion of the population joined the ranks of the middle class, by 1980 the United Methodist minister could not claim much more than a tenuous place in that middle class. Up and down the socioeconomic rankings of clergy by denomination, the same thing has happened since the late 1960s. The practical impact of these changes is that while the minister's job has, if anything, become more difficult since 1960, the economic support provided by congregations to do that job has greatly diminished.

The impact of these economic changes on both clergy households and congregations has been considerable. The institution of the "minister's wife" has all but vanished as a fixture of American church life. To be sure, male and female clergy still often have supportive spouses. However, those spouses now typically work for wages, and it is not unusual for the nonclergy spouse to earn a higher income than the pastor. Protestant congregations can no longer rely, therefore, on a family system whose total adult vocational energies are focused on the life of the church. It is not only the Protestant pastor's household that has changed, however. In U.S. Catholicism the shortage of priestly vocations has meant that fewer and fewer parish priests are stretched over more parishes without benefit of comrades in the rectory—the housekeeper and other priests who provided familial support to generations of earlier priests.

Clearly, all of the economic changes affecting American clergy create stresses for both the clergy and the congregations they serve. One way to understand the pressures on clergy as employees and on parishes as employers is to track what economists would call dependency ratios. The idea is to compare the number of members to the number of pastors employed in congregations. [The following statistics and those in the next two paragraphs are taken from *Yearbook of American and Canadian*

*Churches*, Nashville: Abingdon Press.] Episcopalians in 1965 had 594 members for every parish priest. In 1995, by contrast, membership had dropped much more sharply than the numbers of parochial clergy, so that there were only 313 members supporting each parish priest. No wonder clerical income in the Episcopal church was declining in those years. In the simplest terms, rank-and-file Episcopalians remaining active church members would have needed to become nearly twice as generous to support, at the same real cost, the levels of staffing and personnel that their predecessors enjoyed only 30 years earlier. Episcopalians present an extreme case with their 47 percent decline in membership relative to numbers of clergy.

Episcopal parishes, however, were not alone in experiencing a decline. Congregations of the Evangelical Lutheran Church in America lost 17 percent of their support base. The Presbyterian Church (USA) lost 12 percent. The United Methodist Church managed to maintain a high member-clergy ratio, with only a slight decline from 425 members to 420 members for every ordained minister with a pastoral charge, but only by cutting the number of parish-employed clergy by nearly 20 percent.

Conservative churches were not spared membership losses in relation to pastors. The Lutheran Church–Missouri Synod experienced a loss of 120 members per parish pastor to 462. Of the large denominations, only the Southern Baptist Convention and the Roman Catholic Church experienced increases in the number of members relative to the numbers of parish-based clergy, with gains of 14 percent and 66 percent, respectively; but Roman Catholics improved their ratio through a drastic drop in the number of priests.

## How Churches Think

The problems associated with fair pay for clergy and other church employees is compounded by the way churches and their leaders typically think about compensation. An unfortunate pattern in most of our churches tends to confuse paid-for and paid-to compensation. The former category, paid-for compensation, is the total direct cost of having an employee associated with the organization. Paid-to compensation, on the other hand, refers only to the salary, wages, and, where appropriate, allowances paid to the employee.

It is a fact of life in late 20th-century America that the cost of maintaining employees greatly exceeds the amounts actually paid to them for their services. Expenses related to medical coverage, pensions, education and training, and disability and unemployment insurance coverage all add up. In a wide variety of organizations in all major business sectors, the cost of having an employee on staff amounts to as much as, and sometimes more than, one-and-a-half times the amount of wages paid to that employee. Because even in sophisticated corporations these costs associated with employment are often buried in mountains of spreadsheet data, people are accustomed to thinking about compensation in terms of the narrow category of personal income.

The church may be the only place where large numbers of otherwise sophisticated individuals are faced with the total costs of employment when they consider the personnel portion of the church's budget. A simple example will help make this point more clear. Consider the following package paid to a typical pastor of a midsize church in any one of a number of mainline denominations:

| | |
|---|---|
| Base salary | $28,000 |
| Housing allowance | 12,000 |
| Auto allowance | 3,000 |
| Continuing education | 900 |
| Pension at 12 percent of salary and housing | 4,800 |
| Medical benefits | 6,400 |
| | |
| Total paid-for compensation | $55,100 |

When considering what the minister in the example is paid, many laypeople and even clergy will think in terms of the "package." That is, they will say, "We are paying our minister $55,100." They also compare that $55,100 figure to their own incomes, and say, "That's not a bad salary; at $48,000 a year, I don't make that much." The problem with thinking in these terms is that some items in the package are not income at all; they are the expenses of doing the church's business— namely the auto allowance and the provision for continuing education. Moreover, although it has become more common in recent years to tell employees how much their benefits are costing a company, the price of providing medical insurance coverage and even participation in a pension plan are rarely associated directly with particular employees.

In addition, if we look closely, we will notice that there is no provision for the payment of FICA (Federal Insurance Contributions Act) taxes for the minister, as would be the case for the hypothetical lay member making $48,000 a year. The minister in the example, therefore, will pay approximately $3,000 in Social Security self-employment taxes above and beyond those paid by most employees. Even after the much-vaunted income-tax exclusion for the minister's housing allowance is factored in, the market value of the minister's salary is more on the order of $36,000. Thus instead of a "good" income relative to the lay leader, the minister has only 75 percent of the lay leader's base pay.

Churches have come to use "the package" for two reasons. The first is that many denominational systems require that the terms of clergy employment include stipulated amounts for travel, continuing education, pension, and medical benefits. The second reason is that congregations have an interest in knowing the full cost of their personnel commitments. The problem lies not in knowing these costs, but in confusing the total cost with the garden-variety salaries that the popular media report for various professions or with the incomes received by church members themselves.

A preliminary step for thinking about clergy compensation fairly, therefore, would be for leaders in congregations to disaggregate what is often lumped together. It may even help for leaders in charge of personnel matters to discover what other typical employers in the government, for-profit, and not-for-profit sectors are paying for benefits and other employment costs for the types of work done by the church's members. Having a more realistic basis for a discussion of employee compensation in the churches may not make it easier to raise the money to pay fair wages, but it does tend to take the sting out of discussions that can become heated when fueled by unreality.

If ministers tend to be paid unfairly as the result of a poor understanding of the dimensions of their compensation, lay employees of congregations tend to fare even worse. For more than 50 years, survey after survey has disclosed that most lay employees received no benefits at all other than those mandated by federal and state laws: Social Security and, sometimes, unemployment insurance. What is also known is that male janitors are more likely to receive additional medical or pension benefits as a group than are female secretaries and bookkeepers. Again, this distinction relates to the way churches think. "She doesn't need

benefits; she's covered under her husband's insurance," goes the commonly heard argument. Thus the church becomes a free rider at the expense of women who fill the vast majority of church-secretary and support-staff positions. By contrast, the male janitor, if he is employed full-time, may receive medical benefits precisely because he is perceived as his family's breadwinner.

While several mainline denominations are on record as favoring fairness in employment of lay employees, no nationally organized Christian denomination mandates benefit coverage for congregations' lay employees. These discrepant practices set up a form of economic clericalism whereby clergy get many coverages and considerations not given to those lower on the totem pole. In most employment settings this favoritism would be blatantly illegal, but within the church it persists. Clergy, whose incomes already rise very slowly over the course of their professional careers, find themselves caught in an ethical dilemma since advocating for the coverage of other employees may be detrimental to their own economic well-being.

Churches also think in unusual ways when they assign raises. Pay raises often follow what might be called the least-common-denominator pattern. If a group of lay leaders is sitting around discussing potential staff-salary increases and someone says, "I know that inflation is 4 percent, but times are tough and I only got a 2 percent increase this year," the group may tend to follow that thinking and give clergy and other staff a 2 percent raise so as not to offend the church member who is experiencing a subinflationary increase this year. This kind of thinking is even more likely to be the case when a church is having difficulty making ends meet. The "times are tough, so we all must sacrifice" theory tends to assign the greater burden of required sacrifices to those employed by the church.

Churches in wealthier, suburban areas tend to give bigger raises to their church staffs, in part because their members experience salary increases. The irony is that the church whose members experience less upward social mobility may not love its pastor any less, nor the wealthier church love its minister any more. The compensation, therefore, may bear little or no relation to employee effectiveness or the difficulty of the work performed. It goes without saying then that most congregations are due for a change in the way they think about how they value and compensate clergy, other professional staff and supporting employees.

# How the Church Ought to Think About Paying Its Servants

How ought the church to think about paying its servants? If the problem lies at least in part in the thoughtless application of principles that don't fit the situation, then we might begin by thinking about some principles that do fit.

The first principle is that church employment practices are inevitably a *model for* and a *model of* the church. They are a model for the church insofar as the way we treat ministers, choir directors, secretaries, and custodians in relation to employment and compensation becomes—whether we like it or not—a normative model for the members of the congregation. If we underpay the pastor and choir director year in and year out and rationalize that they are paid less because they have chosen a self-giving, altruistic profession, then we are saying that people who choose self-giving, altruistic professions do not deserve to be paid according to the standards of fairness that apply to most members of society. If a congregation provides medical and pension benefits to its pastors and music director but not to its secretary, bookkeeper, or custodians, it is saying that some kinds of people in some kinds of jobs don't deserve job-based access to health care or security in old age.

Given the fact that a church's employment practices are a model for a congregation's members in other parts of life, congregational leadership ought to think carefully about whether its practices are communicating norms and values consistent with the congregation's view of the Christian life and of how people should relate to one another in economic matters. If a congregation wishes to press for social justice in the working world, discrimination in its own employment practices will vitiate its testimony.

But we have also said that the churches' employment practices are a model *of* the church: *Whatever* practices the church uses, those practices will disclose something about the contemporary character of the church and its members. The way people think about supporting their church employees will come out in their practices just as the way corporations think about their employees comes out in their employment practices. In short, a church's employment practices provide a living witness both to a congregation's view of the world as it should be and its view of the world as it is.

The second principle guiding how churches ought to think about paying their servants is this: The church needs to adopt practices that it believes should be followed in the workplace and not simply those it can get away with. If it is possible to obtain the services of a female minister for less money than the services of a comparable male minister, the church needs to ask itself whether it is right to pay women ministers less. If it is offensive to think of paying female surgeons less than male surgeons for similar surgical procedures, then the church must apply this moral sense about what is fair to its own affairs. Churches have been in the forefront of decrying such practices as child labor. When they have resisted these practices, they have almost always done so by rejecting the ultimate laissez-faire argument that children were willing to work for the amount offered. Anytime someone in a church context says, "We can get So-and-So for x dollars," church leaders should be attuned to the possibility that they are using this same kind of reasoning.

This principle is not a counsel to perfection, as if the church should not employ anyone without offering ideal wages, superb benefits, and excellent working conditions. Instead it is a plea that the church not use any standard inferior to the best practices of other employers in the prevailing economy. If a university, a corporation, or a fast-food chain can offer its clerical and other service-sector employees some form of health-care coverage, what is the church doing when it refuses to try?

Here again we return to the model of the commonwealth and ask what difference it might make for churches' employment practices to think about collective Christianity in these terms. The notion of commonwealth reorients the way we think about our economic relations. We normally think about ourselves as consumers. The question we ask as consumers is "What can I get for my money?" To be a member of the commonwealth, however, is to be not principally a consumer but rather a citizen. In a commonwealth one asks different questions. First of all, when one is a part-owner in an enterprise, one asks, "What should I do with my resources?" When one thinks as a citizen, one asks, "How by a particular action are my fellow citizens and I enriched or impoverished?"

Most important, when one thinks in terms of commonwealth, the economic losses and gains are understood to be shared to the extent that it is impossible to make others bear the costs of something you want without experiencing a diminishment of the community to which you want to belong. In these terms, paying employees of the church unfairly

with respect to either the Christian community or to prevailing market conditions diminishes the congregation, even if the employee will accept the wages and benefits. Why? Because this kind of unfairness amounts to a refusal to share, undermining the character of the congregation as the sharing community. Curiously, thinking in terms of commonwealth may mean that pastors sometimes will not receive the kinds of raises they would like because of a need to maintain solidarity with their members and fellow church servants. On the other hand, the relative poverty that emerges from communal solidarity is greatly to be preferred to the tenuous wealth that comes from thoughtlessly pandering to the worst market practices.

### The Case of the Pastor's Pay

Let us now turn to some cases in which the principles can be applied. What, for example, about the earlier question: To whom is the pastor to be compared? Is it to the teacher, the principal, the superintendent, the doctor, the lawyer, the day laborer? We might be tempted to answer the question on the basis of some external criteria such as the number of years of graduate education required to hold the position. And surely the pastor's pay ought to have something to do with the ascribed social value of his or her work and where else these skills might be deployed, including other congregations within the faith tradition.

Yet thinking of the congregation as a commonwealth forces us to ask who the minister is in relation to the commonwealth's citizens. Is the minister one of them or a stranger hired to do a job? Being a hireling, it is important to note, does not necessarily mean that one will be paid an inferior wage. We pay certain professionals—doctors and real estate agents, to name but two—considerable sums to do jobs for us. Still, the hireling is in a functional relationship with the employer. We tend not to make those who are in functional relationships part of our families, part of us, part of the fabric of our lives, except in exceptional circumstances. However, the relationship between pastor and people, at its best, is not purely functional. Therefore, the most critical question a congregation can ask itself is the following: "Is the minister to be one of us?" Conversely, the most important question for the minister to ask is, "Am I one of these people?"

From the increased propensity of congregations to sack ministers at will, one suspects that too often one or both of the parties are answering that the minister is not one with the body of believers. From its earliest days, however, the church of Jesus Christ has been at its healthiest when its leadership was fundamentally identified with the people of God as a whole and not with a special caste set over against the laity. From the perspective of commonwealth, these questions revolve around the minister's relationship to people:

- Do the laity pay the minister enough to live among them? If church members rent their housing, can he rent a similar dwelling? If they own their homes, can she afford a similar home?
- Do they pay according to their own means and according to the needs of their pastor?
- Do they pay enough not to breed resentment, and not so much as to breed feelings of superiority?

I can already hear some pastors raising objections. Some will say, "But what of the highly skilled minister called to serve a congregation of poor people subsisting largely on day labor?" Others will object that no minister ought to be paid as much as the average upper-class parishioner of some Episcopal, Congregational, Reformed, and Presbyterian churches. My answer is that clearly the extended-family relationships between congregations of Christians ought to be more just, and that the wealthy should help supply the needs of the poor. Yet I would also point out that it is a rare congregation at the lower end of the socioeconomic spectrum, whose faith is alive and membership vital, that cannot attract from among its supporters sufficient funds to meet the needs of its pastor. Far more common is the pastor who, because of economic distance from the congregation, leads a life of quiet desperation, becoming progressively alienated from the people and looking for a parish that may compensate its pastoral leadership in a way that truly invites the minister to be one with the congregation.

**Paying the Lay Employee**

The second case is that of the lay employee. Many of the basic principles, like fairness and comparable worth, apply as they do to clergy

compensation. And yet, there are differences in context to consider. While the question "Is she one of us and are we one with her?" is a relevant question when applied by a congregation to its minister, it is sometimes a poor question when applied to secretarial and custodial employees. Some lay employees feel called to the work they do; others do not. An employee who is not religiously called to serve a church ought to be treated more as a sojourner than as a community member. The sojourner in biblical times was singled out for special notice precisely because it was tempting to take care of one's own people but to take advantage of outsiders. Strangers and those who worked in the community without being members of it needed to be treated with justice and fairness, lest the community diminish itself by maltreatment of others.

What does being fair and just mean in the context of working with nonministerial employees? It means being generous, not with respect to all possible employment contexts, but in relation to the one within which the church operates. We can draw a comparison between working for a church and working in one of the guest-worker programs of the Western European countries. Some of these guest-worker programs are regarded as generous by the workers who report back on their experiences to family members in their home countries. Most programs are not so well regarded.

The congregation is like a commonwealth in this respect: To the extent that it wishes to be regarded as a good place to work, its objective ought to be to receive a good report in the home contexts of its employees. This is not so easy to implement as an unequivocal rule that health and pension benefits must always be paid to service employees of churches. Fairness may mean paying more benefits, or taking into account particular employees' family benefits and adjusting compensation in tandem with benefits (within the law, of course) to leave the employees best off in their own eyes. The clear implication of dealing with employees from outside the congregation's fold is that attention must be paid to what seems just to the employees. Fairness is a two-part concept, consisting of the perceptions of both the employer and the employee. However fair we as a congregation feel we are being as employers, it still matters how we are perceived by our employees. On the whole, therefore, if we must err, let us err on the side of generosity.

# Exercise

## How Much Should We Pay?

It is said that a just situation in human affairs exists when all parties to
an agreement would freely consent to it in advance of knowing what
role they would play. That is, a just situation would exist between the
wealthy and the poor if all people were able to agree as to how the
wealthy should treat the poor before knowing whether they themselves
would be fated to be rich or poor. This exercise asks you likewise to
imagine both sides of an economic relationship. Choose a particular role
among the staff positions in your congregation. It can be the minister,
the choir director, the secretary, the custodian, or any other employee.
Now, without knowing whether you will fill the role or be responsible
for paying the person in the role, decide on a fair amount to pay the
individual doing the job. What kinds of benefits should be offered or
paid? How did you arrive at the wages and benefits you believe to be
fair for the position? Talk with others in your congregation who have
gone through the same exercise and compare their results with your own.
What do you find when you compare results? What do those results have
to say about your congregation's current employment practices and the
ways in which those practices may need to change?

# CHAPTER 9

# Where Theology Matters: Faith and Money in the Life of the Generous Individual

Throughout this book, I've been quite clear about how I think generous saints behave. By this point, we should all be able to recognize such a person. The question remains, "How do I become a generous saint?"

Becoming clear about our money, our work, the economy, our mission, our stewardship, our congregational practices—all of these are important way stations toward becoming more generous and holy. But now in the final chapter I want to turn to the project of personal and group transformation; our move is from questions of "what?" to "how?" That is, we know what a generous person looks like, but we desperately want to know how to become one.

People can become only the sort of people they can imagine themselves becoming. I believe that most of our failures to live generous lives are not failures generated by lack of knowledge or will, but the result of too little imagination. We see others as saintly. We see others as generous. But knowing our own shortcomings all too well, we fail to picture our lives as candidates for generous sainthood.

Often we are amazed at how good someone is. In the role of pastor, I have had the experience of being utterly stunned by a life story related by an older person that is hard to listen to and yet inspiring at the same time. You probably know the sort of story I'm talking about. One thing after another befell the individual and her family—the Great Depression, illness, a son lost in the Pacific—and still they took in the orphan child their minister mentioned in prayer one Sunday. Or they sent their money off to missionaries in China when the machine-parts plant upon which their livelihood depended faced imminent closure. People have lived those kinds of generous, almost heroic lives not only in the past. I have known people with crippling arthritis to struggle out of bed to

prepare food to take to the bedside of a friend with the flu. What do I make, I sometimes wonder, of the woman who has lost three sons to AIDS and yet delights in every child she meets as though no hope is impossible? These people are just as saintly as any I read about in Butler's *Lives of the Saints*. Still, the question remains, how did they get that way?

## How Shall I Live? What Shall I Do?

By this point, it should be clear that being a generous individual in a community of saints is not easy work. Concerns for personal financial security, the ways in which our best life-plans are often overtaken by events, and the sheer difficulty of maintaining community with others who share our commitments all make living the life of a generous saint difficult. Developing a set of values and then living in accord with those values is, however, the ethical task of the Christian life. Ethics is always about the questions "How shall I (or we) live?" and "What shall I (or we) do?" The ethics of generous sainthood forces us to turn from ethics' usual emphasis on the second question to the first—from the question of "doing" to the question of "living." Questions of "doing" always have a short-term dimension, and sainthood is, finally, a long-term proposition. As such, the goal of generous sainthood impels us to conduct our moral reasoning less on the basis of decisions and more on the basis of narrative. In this chapter, I will label this alternative, constructive mode of ethical discourse "narrative ethics."

To understand the value of a narrative approach to ethics, we first must see the limitations of how we are accustomed to approaching ethical questions. What we do with our lives and money, time, sexuality, or talents is often depicted as a matter of decision. We decide to increase our pledge by 10 percent. We decide not to start an affair but to be faithful in our marriage. We decide to volunteer on a series of Saturdays to help build a Habitat for Humanity house. Or so it seems. A decision-based understanding of ethics locates the crucial point for understanding why people do what they do at the moment when a decision seems to be required.

There are different versions of decision-based ethics. In rule-based ethics the moral actor is expected to apply rules and principles derived

from the Christian faith and rational thought to particular situations.
Thus, the rule "Thou shalt not kill" stays the hand of the person moved
to fury by the outrageous conduct of another. The rule "Always do unto
others as you would have done unto to you" likewise can result in someone's always putting a few coins into the cups held forth by the homeless
on city street corners.

By contrast, consequentialism still focuses on the point of decision
but argues that the proper weighing of the consequences of a given decision determines the morality of the choices made in the situation.
Thus, in the classic example of consequentialist reasoning, murdering
Adolf Hitler may be justified even for a Christian, since the conse-
quence of allowing Hitler to continue killing represents a greater evil
than that of taking Hitler's life. When they move from murder to mundane matters, such as whether to increase one's pledge by 10 percent,
however, consequentialists have a more difficult time carrying out their
program of moral reasoning. Why is this? Because the consequences of a
small change are so difficult to discern.

The more basic problem with these decision-based forms of moral
reasoning is their focus on decisions themselves. Decisions are necessary
points of a life, but they are not *the* point of a life. A human life in its
totality is its own subject. That is, no one regards his or her own life
simply as a stage for a series of right decisions. Instead, all the decisions
or turning points are episodes in what is really important—the individual life itself. Thus ethics ought to be concerned with the totality of
a person's life, his or her character, experiences, values, and aspirations;
in short, his or her entire story, however simple or complex. An ethics
that concentrates on a life story in relation to other life stories may be
properly called narrative ethics. As we shall see, it is a form of reasoning that is especially well suited to helping people come to terms as
individuals and in faith groups with issues of faith, money, faithfulness,
and generosity.

## An Adventure in Narrative Ethics

If ethics is the appraisal of conduct, then narrative ethics is the appraisal
of conduct in the context of the narrative (or story) of an individual's
life (or the life of a people). When we do ethical analysis from the perspective of narrative, we avoid becoming trapped in abstract discussions

about duty, obligations, or principles in isolation from people and their problems. How a person or a people ought to live is properly considered within the context of the story of the life or lives in question. Imagine the following:

> My mother taught me it was always a terrible thing to lie, but when the Gestapo came looking for the neighbor I had hid in my attic, I believed that she would understand I did not owe the truth to the evil man at the door as much as I owed protection to the good man in my attic.

Already, we can see that the truth of the narrative with its conflicting principles (never lie, always do good, honor your mother, love your neighbor, etc.) is more profound than any of the principles themselves, taken in isolation. Narrative ethics is, therefore, a commonsense way of determining what is good from the complexity of life itself and not from either principles or utilitarianism derived from some unreal abstraction.

We practice narrative ethics in our own lives the same way we appraise the moral conduct, character, virtue, and life-choices of those we read about in novels and biographies. Think about how you read a story about someone else. As the story unfolds, you can spot the good characters, even when they falter. This kind of observation proves to be a very helpful way of proceeding, since if we can see someone else's life as more than the sum of good and bad decisions, then we can understand our own lives as possessing the same character, together with the potential for positive change. Compared to decision-based ethics, narrative ethics entails a longer view. We need not wait for a life's completion to begin practicing narrative ethics. Rather, the subject of our ethical inquiry is a life in the process of completion.

Narrative ethics is not self-justification in disguise. Indeed, in the telling of a story about what we did and why we did it, we lay ourselves open to challenge by hearers. We contextualize the things we do, and our hearers accept the account or say something like, "No, I think you are kidding yourself." Out of that crafting and recrafting of our story and stories, we come to self-understanding. Nor is self-understanding the end of ethics done in a narrative framework. For it to be ethics, something else must be added. With self-understanding come moments of insight that give us pride. Other moments bring sadness about things we

wish had gone differently. In a faith context, these insights can be occasions for atonement and for seeking forgiveness. They may also bring us to moments of repentance (or turning around), when we join insight into how we have lived with a realistic commitment to live differently.

A narrated ethics looks and functions with respect both to the past and to the future. It functions retrospectively, taking this basic form:

*I did thus and so, because I believed/felt/thought this and that.*

The ethical narrative also functions prospectively:

*I will do thus and such because I believe/feel/think this and that.*

The narrative necessarily splits between past and future, for it is not just an explanation of what is past but also a construction of what is hoped for (and feared) in the future. We should expect to see several meta-plot options. They include

1. *Conversion*: A rejection of significant aspects of past life and future life is premised on repentance for the lives we've lived.
2. *Progress toward holiness*: Our future lives in these accounts look like extensions of the best parts of our lives to date.
3. *A struggle with sainthood*: We realize that we will ever be incomplete, yet ours will be a tensive life—one that holds in tension who we are with what we know the good to be.

Appraising the conduct and quality of a life cannot, of course, be done in real time. In real time, one can either live a life or observe one. Even if one were able to observe someone's life closely, it would take other people attending to the context of that life to be able to see what was happening to an individual. Moreover, not all moments are equally instructive of a person's character, essential qualities, and personality. It is necessary, therefore, to take some shortcuts—to discern the relevant details of a person's life, relationships, and conduct. That is how philosophers and theologians began to abstract ethical principles, virtues, and rules from real life in the first place.

I contend, however, that we have tended to go too far, to become too abstract, and have produced accounts far too thin of what is ethically

relevant. We have looked at critical decisions and principles as indicators of whether people are good or bad. As we tell our stories, we are still looking for critical turning points and informative events, but we are also examining formative practices, and the cultures in which people are formed. In short, we are looking for a richer way of describing what matters and why, what happened and why.

Narrative ethics offers another strength to those who would be generous saints. It recognizes from the beginning that stories intersect. Standard ethics tends to suggest that people decide and act autonomously according to their values and interests. Narrative ethics insists that people are connected—to thoughts, communities, traditions, practices, ways of thinking, and other moral actors. People need to be the subjects of their own ethical narratives, but they are never the only subjects. An individual is never the only actor.

But what of God as an actor? Part of the promise of narrative ethics, as *Christian* ethics, is that it allows for a reintroduction of God as a character, and of grace, providence, tragedy, evil, redemption, and even eschatology as themes. Decision-based, ruled-based, and even virtue ethics (in which the ethical life is one characterized by the cultivation of virtues and the decultivation of vices) cannot do the same, for by themselves they locate activity in a moral agent or agents. That God has already acted in history is mostly assumed, in these other moral theories, to be irrelevant to the immediate decisions at hand.

The challenge of being and becoming a generous saint is to tell a true story about oneself becoming generous and holy and then to live that story through to completion. I have already indicated that these stories can take a number of plot forms. Moreover, they can take on as many particular twists as there are people to live them. But lest one think that living one of these stories is impossible, boring, or even easy, it is worth paying attention to stories of the lives of the saints before us.

## Difficult Lives

Saints' lives are often difficult lives, but they are lives in which God is present. If we are seeking to become more holy and generous, then exploration of difficult and saintly lives is one of the helpful practices in which our congregations might engage. To explore the life of Martin

Luther King, Jr., or an apostle like Peter helps us understand how
Christian disciples may manage to do the right thing despite having
given in to the impulses to marital infidelity on the one hand and to
denial of one's relationship with Christ on the other.

The further one gets into the biography of *Catholic Worker* founder
Dorothy Day, the less saintly she seems, if by saintly we assume a life
free of uncharitable thoughts toward others, a life of self-denial, and a
life of cheerful giving to others. The example of Mother Teresa of
Calcutta in our time lulls us into a flat conception of holiness. But with
Dorothy Day, we meet a figure who struggles with a desire for privacy, a
love for people who let her down, and a commitment to giving that is
not always rewarded by either cheerfulness or joy. As such, the life of a
generous saint becomes more conceivable for all of us who wake up
thinking we are just normal.

Perhaps no life of a Christian disciple has been better told than that
of Augustine of Hippo. Certainly no autobiography has been more often
read over a longer period of time than that of Augustine's *Confessions*.
Part of the attraction of Augustine's narrative is that at many points he
seems just like us at our worst. At other points he is almost unbelievably
callous, dense, or selfish. As readers encounter Augustine the sinner and
Augustine the saint, their imaginations are engaged by the possibility
that their own redemption may not be impossible. Indeed, one of the
20th century's best-loved spiritual classics, Thomas Merton's *The Seven
Storey Mountain*, can be read as one man's finding his life and calling
in another man's (in this case Augustine's) story. In plot and structure
there are critical similarities between the *Confessions* and *The Seven
Storey Mountain*.

But perhaps even more important, Merton's autobiography has also
inspired millions who have seen their own life stories told in a story of
another. Thus life stories, particularly narratives of difficult lives, have
the ability to communicate more profound truths about Christian discipleship and sanctification (that is, the process by which one becomes
more holy, more saintly) than do rule books, checklists, and even the
best expository sermons. With their rough edges and unresolved plots,
the difficult life stories carry a ring of truth that nonetheless provides
hope that we too might yet be saints.

## The Uses of Narrative in Shaping Our Lives

In all the great lives we find aspects and incidents in which an honest autobiographer could have taken no pride. Yet these scenes are important to the narrative, for their inclusion constructs a Christian ethics of perseverance. The idea that "you can do it too" is a theme that endures, as Pilgrim and Faithful persevered in John Bunyan's *A Pilgrim's Progress*. The best-loved Christian spiritual literature is in the form of narrative, beginning with the Pentateuch in the Old Testament and the gospels in the New Testament. The lesson for the would-be saint is reiterated again and again: God is always faithful; people are less so, but for those who strive to be faithful, God is merciful and just.

When I was a graduate student and working at the Princeton University Chapel, the dean of the chapel, Frederick Borsch, instituted a program titled "What Matters to Me and Why." The purpose of the series was to allow professors to come clean with their students outside the classroom and truly profess what they cared about, what motivated their lives, and the commitments for which they would be willing to be tested. The chapel staff had a difficult time on Sunday mornings getting many students out for worship. But on Tuesday or Thursday nights, when the professors stood under the spotlight and professed, there was not a seat to be had in the chapel gathering room. And sometimes there was not a dry eye in the house. These undergraduates, like all of us, loved to hear a good story. Better yet, they were moved and enriched by the hearing of an important story. Moreover, in hearing the professors' accounts of their lives, students were helped in imagining the stories of their own lives.

A note of caution: With its emphasis on story, narrative ethics is easily confused with a form of mostly narcissistic show-and-tell. Most of us have seen the latter in sermons at one time or another since the narrative form of preaching became popular: I tell my story, and I invite you to think about your story, and we try together to see God's story. That's not narrative ethics. Narrative ethics is, first, a method of richer analysis and second, a mode of discourse about our lives and about our shared life.

Narrative forms offer the only way to make ourselves understood about some matters. Take moral ambiguity, for instance. By telling our stories we can say "I messed up, OK?" and mean both halves of that

sentence. We can expose our vulnerability for having done something which, in retrospect, we wish we had not done, and yet plead for forgiveness and acceptance—indeed, for reassurance that we are still basically OK. Narrative ethics sets the framework for saying more than "her life was right" or "her life was wrong." That is the kind of game we like to play in public discourse and in the press, both in my hometown and in yours. Living in the South has helped me see how a life might be both praiseworthy and tragically blind. Consider those white Southerners who tried to live the lives of good Christians in pre-civil-rights days, who displayed love to all who came their way and charity for those who needed it, black or white, yet who defended the institution of segregation that had been taught to them. Most lives have similar features of moral ambiguity.

We can also highlight decisive, constructive moral moments through narrative. It is only in the context of a whole story that a turning point can be seen for what it is. Martin Luther King, Jr., had a moral moment that for him explained all others in his discipleship. During the Montgomery bus boycott, his house was firebombed. After the fire was out, after the authorities had left, he sat down at the kitchen table and wondered what he had gotten himself into. In his exhaustion, he experienced reassurance and the power of God. Each time he recounted the story for reporters and in his books, the incident took on greater and greater significance. By looking back to the "kitchen conversion," he even explained his discipleship to himself. As we look to narrate our lives, we need likewise to listen for the small turns in the story that direct the flow of the whole story.

Narrative ethics is also a form of discourse about things that matter to us. When my father's leukemia went out of control and he knew death was nearby, if not imminent, he began to ask friends to tell him stories. He often relayed to me the stories he was told. They almost always had both a point and a moral. Yet they conveyed in their telling more than a summary point would have conveyed. The very fact of what stories were chosen allowed the tellers to say to my father things that had gone unsaid between friends. It allowed friends to become honest and vulnerable with one another, without breaking down.

Perhaps two ministers should be able to say straight out to one another, "If you die, I will miss you deeply, but you need to know I have been watching you all these years, and I and countless others around our

presbytery have been touched by you." But two men in their early 60s—
even sensitive-minister types—just don't say it that way, even if they
mean it. Stories allow us to say what our hearts know. That's why we tell
so many stories to children and why we ought to use them to understand
and reshape our lives.

Narratives are meant to be shared. Is there a story without a telling
of that story? Like the tree falling in the forest and the question of
whether there is prelinguistic thought, this question may be, I think,
philosophically insoluble. For Christians, however, there seems to be no
worthwhile story that doesn't get shared. Narrative absent the ritual of
storytelling can be said not to exist for the community. It is your song
perhaps, but it is not a Christian song until it is shared with a community
of Christians. It is impossible to be a disciple alone on a sustained basis.
One's witness either gets out and finds hearers, or it dissolves.

Sharing narratives communally also enables a people to arrive at a
sense of what is normative—something that ought to be done. The doing
of ethics in a Christian context requires that we engage in constant conversation. It happens when we say, "I did this for these reasons. . . . I am
this way because I value . . ."—and then struggle with fellow Christians
who hear us and believe part of what we say and yet challenge us to
redraft our stories in both the retelling and in the scripting for the future
that we live the next day, week, and month. The claim that narrative
ethics is tied to living the Christian life is not an exclusive claim, as
though people of other traditions did not live their stories and narrate
their lives according to their traditions. Nevertheless, it is especially
true that Christians are a people of a shared story called the Gospel,
which, retold in a variety of forms, including gospels and letters, is
much more complex than a merely propositional faith (believe X, and
then Y will happen).

Small virtues, exercised consistently, add up to a pattern of virtue.
How often in our experience do great outcomes hinge on small beginnings? To see how generous and holy lives are, in fact, built over time,
our ethical frame of reference needs to be long-term. This is especially,
but not exclusively, true in regard to issues of faith, money, and generosity. Perseverence is a virtue for a reason. Perhaps nowhere else can we
see more clearly the limits of taking too short-term a view of our lives
than in the problems that youth experience. Take, for example, the
problems of violence among the young or teen pregnancy. Again and

again when we ask, "Why did this tragedy happen?" the answers we hear are cast within incredibly short time-frames:

- "She dissed me so I burned her apartment. I need to respect myself. If a man ain't got no respect for hisself, he ain't nobody."
- "I killed him because I know he would kill me."
- "I dunno. I guess I just went ahead and did it because I wanted to have a baby who would love me."

All of these quotes from teenagers are moral accounts of the way things were as the teenagers saw them at the time. Most of us as adults can readily see how tragically shortsighted these perspectives are. There is more to self-respect than an immediate response to perceived disrespect. Death is final and—when one is young—usually avoidable. A baby changes one's life forever. We can see the teenagers' accounts as moral tales told by people with insufficiently long moral horizons. We know intuitively that the momentary interruptions of youthful conflict and disrespect are hurdles to be lived through, surmounted, and overcome, and not the main events. Perseverance, triumph over adversity, courage in the face of peer pressure, even the courage to change one's mind—these are the themes one engages when one considers one's life on a grander scale.

But we, like our youth, love dramatic conflict too much. Films like *West Side Story* and *An Officer and a Gentleman* and *Boyz N the Hood* are too attractive to us. *Driving Miss Daisy* and *Babette's Feast* are less exciting, but which lives would we really prefer to live—long, rich ones or short ones punctuated by violence? We must learn to appreciate longer stories if we are to live full and generous lives. Longer stories are told by survivors and saints.

## Finding the Truth When Stories Conflict

One last objection to narratives as the basis for ethics is that evil people can tell stories too. This observation overlooks the fact that we don't have to credit all stories equally. I, for one, would argue that one credits a narrative that the author genuinely believes to be true and one that disinterested but informed observers and listeners also believe to be true.

Discrepancy poses no special difficulties. Indeed, the doing of ethics comes in two parts. The first is the living of the story and the composition of the narrative; the second is the conversation that ensues when one party's account of the story conflicts with another party's account. In the Christian community we might call this process "holding someone accountable." What is it we hold one another accountable to? It is nothing less than the veracity of our stories before God. Confession and forgiveness, two critical aspects of our Christian relationship with God, are based in truth. Sometimes accountability comes when someone else tells a truth we don't want told; sometimes it's a truth we need to discover within a confessing and forgiving community.

A Baptist pastor in Miami, Florida, named George McRae has a chemical-dependency response team within his congregation. The response team is prepared to serve as the Christian community that enables addicts to rewrite the life stories that they had been living until they reached the point of wanting to repent. The community support is vital, for at moments of difficult change—including those surrounding the issues of money and faithfulness—we are generally unable to reorient our lives by sheer force of will. The admonition "Go and sin no more" is rewritten in such faithful communities to read, "Come with us and sin no more." In George McRae's church, addicts show up with a story that is in conflict with the one they would like to tell about themselves as children of God. It is in the power of a community of faith that the presenting narratives can be reconciled and people can be healed. This kind of power is also present, if untapped, in most Christian congregations. The question remains: Do we want to risk telling a faith-and-money story in the hope that we can be transformed?

## Experiments in Generosity

One thing we can do to get a grip on generosity through doing narrative ethics is to think and talk about other people's stories. Do you know any generous people? Tell their life stories as best you can. Now analyze the stories and the people in them. What are the characters like? What makes them the way they are? We also need to work honestly on our own stories. Think about yourself and your story. When have you been generous? When have you been selfish? How has each gesture felt?

What response has your behavior prompted in others? What motivates your best self?

Talking about the past is useful as far as it goes, but I have discovered that one of the most valuable exercises for one who seeks self-understanding and transformation to live more generously and faithfully is to script one's life the way one would like to live it. About five years ago, I began to teach a seminary course called "Faith and Money." The course covered a lot of history, ethics, and theology, but in the end I was interested in seeing how students pulled together what they'd learned for themselves. For the final class assignment I asked each student to write a letter on the occasion of his or her 70th birthday to a loved one. The students were to look back upon their lives and communicate what they thought was important about the way they had lived, particularly in regard to issues of faith and money.

I will never forget the papers from that class assignment. The theological reasoning was some of the most natural and authentic I had ever read. Some students wrote quite beautifully about conversions that had already happened in their way of thinking about material life. One, a woman who had been through a messy divorce, wrote about how she had discovered that what really mattered was the simple pleasure of enjoying a meal with her teenage son at his favorite restaurant. It was not an expensive restaurant. It was not even (to my way of thinking) a great restaurant, but dining out was something they did together in post-nuclear-family days that taught them the transcendent joy of a new kind of togetherness. The cars, the country-club memberships, even the family's revered status in the church, had not brought the pleasure that a small amount of material and a large amount of shared love brought.

Another student, then in her early 30s, wrote about herself as a 70-year-old, describing the lifestyle choices she and her husband had made to have the careers to which they felt called and not the ones that others had suggested would fit them. She wrote of the sacrifices of time and sometimes of opportunities that they made for the sake of being together more of the time. And most tellingly, I think, she wrote about how they had stayed in their first, somewhat small home, and paid it off without moving up in the real-estate world, so that they could give ever-increasing amounts to church-related hunger and development efforts overseas. They also volunteered for these same causes. Their values had served them well over time, and their lives, while not always easy, were

deeply satisfying and mostly regret-free. If they had reached age 70 with less stuff than their brothers and sisters, then at least they knew why. They hadn't consumed foolishly but had spent their modest resources and their lives consistently with the faith that had brought them together as a couple in their college years. This story, told before it was lived, had an important function in the life of the writer and her husband. It allowed them to clarify their views about what they believed and how they wanted to live.

Another student pictured herself as an elderly aunt leaving some money and wisdom behind for her nephew. In her letter, she explained that she always knew that the boy's parents would see that he had the material necessities, but that he might have noticed that she always gave him books, lessons, camp tuition, or something else to stretch his mind. She believed in education as an extension of what God had given. It meant a great deal to her in her life, and now she hoped he too would use this money and his own to improve his mind and to give back to the human community in a celebration of the life of the mind.

The dreams for the future of these and other seminarians were all unique, but in no case did the future sound as though it absolutely required a condo on the beach or a houseboat in the Florida Keys. Those things played a minor role in the lives people wanted to lead. As they pictured themselves at 70, they wanted to be viewed as generous, and they wanted to be seen as faithful to God and their understanding of the Christian message. The impressive thing for me as the teacher was that they all knew ways that *they* could live to demonstrate those qualities and commitments. Reaching deep inside of who they knew themselves to be, they could articulate what it looked like for them to be "generous saints." Note, however, that their assignment was not to write how they *became* generous saints. It was, rather, to write a faith-and-money autobiographical letter. They were only to talk about the unspeakably close —their personal faith and what they had done with their money. Yet, as the stories unfolded, the students turned out to be (potentially) very generous and holy people.

Earlier I indicated that we do one another moral favors by testing each other's narratives. My students were not asked to do that for one another. Still, I was surprised by how "in character" these future stories sounded for the individuals who wrote them. Their narratives passed the plausibility test. The students did not share their narratives with one

another. But after reading their stories, I urged each student to share the story now with someone who could hold them accountable to their vision of the future, to help them "live the story" they wrote. I also urged them to put a copy away in a safe place and to visit it occasionally, especially, if they were so fortunate, on the occasion of their 70th birthdays.

I commend the writing of one's life from the future backward as a practice of spiritual and ethical discernment. I am even more convinced of its utility after working on such narratives with others and writing one myself. In writing about the life I wanted to live, I found a new truth in the words of the prophet Micah:

> He has told you, O mortal, what is good;
> and what does the LORD require of you
> but to do justice, and to love kindness,
> and to walk humbly with your God? (Mic. 6:8).

The truth was this: We already know what is good; we've already been told by God. Our task is to live out the justice, the kindness, and the humility in our lives with God and our fellow creatures. Now I challenge you, the reader, to find the unique story that you can live that has those elements—justice, love of kindness, and walking humbly before God. Find the story, share it with others in your congregation, and be transformed by it as you live. Then, though challenges certainly await and insecurities will threaten to derail you, prepare to take your place among the generous saints we are called to become.

## Exercises

### Generous Saints I Have Known

Tell a group in the congregation the story of one person you know personally who fits the category "generous saint." Be sure to tell your listeners why you think that person exemplifies the ideal of faithful generosity. As you hear others' stories, listen for common themes, sources of strength, and life patterns that emerge. Talk with the group about what these commonalities suggest for your lives and for your life together.

**My Life as a Generous Saint**

Pick a point in the future from which you would like to look back and write how it is that you, despite all your faults, became a person others would see as faithful and generous. Make sure the story you tell is plausible. Share it with a partner, friend, or spouse. With God's help, live the story.